100
THINGS TO
KNOW ABOUT

NUMBERS, COMPUTERS & CODING

Written by
Alice James, Eddie Reynolds,
Minna Lacey, Rose Hall and Alex Frith

Illustrated by
Federico Mariani, Parko Polo
and Shaw Nielsen

Layout and design by
Lenka Hrehova, Freya Harrison,
Tilly Kitching and Jenny Offley

What's this book about?

This book is all about numbers, computers and coding, how they are used and how they are developing all the time.

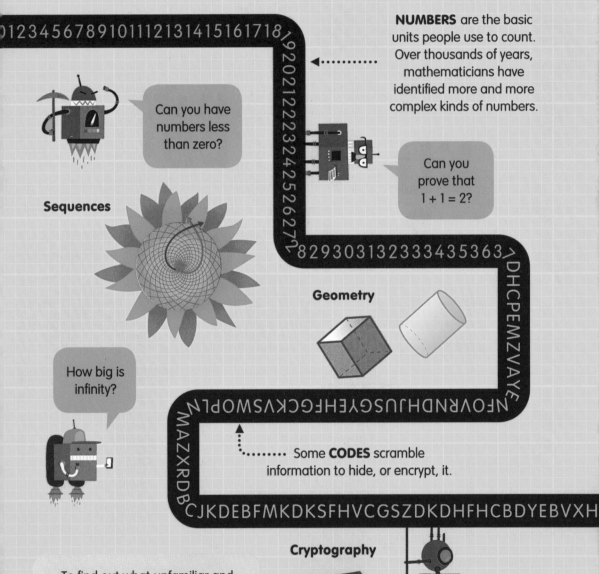

0123456789101112131415161718192021222324252627 28293031323334353637

NUMBERS are the basic units people use to count. Over thousands of years, mathematicians have identified more and more complex kinds of numbers.

Can you have numbers less than zero?

Sequences

Can you prove that 1 + 1 = 2?

Geometry

How big is infinity?

Some **CODES** scramble information to hide, or encrypt, it.

To find out what unfamiliar and technical words in this book mean, go to the glossary on pages 120-123.

Cryptography

How are secret codes created and broken?

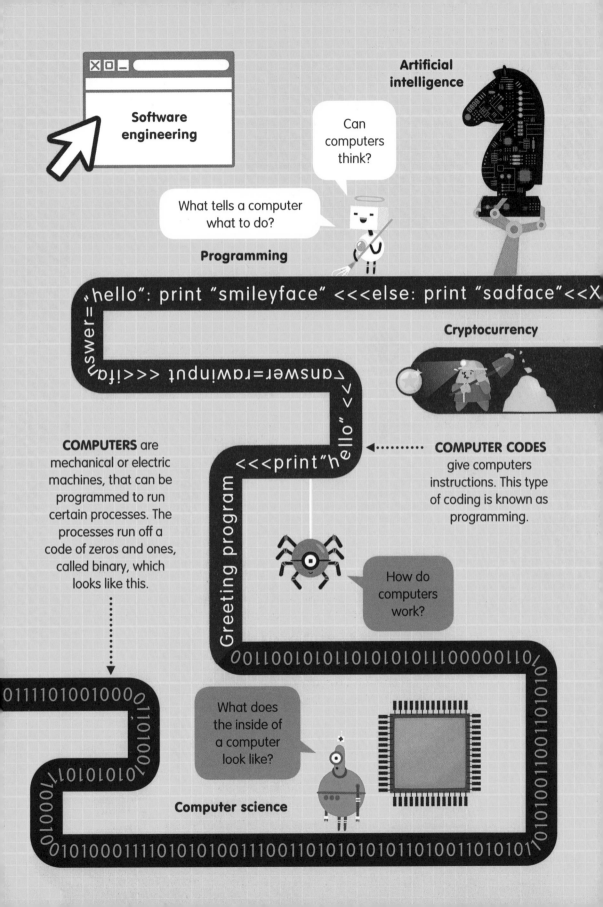

1 01001000 01101001...

is "Hi" in computer language.

The only language any computer understands is one called **machine code**. It's written with just two symbols: 0 and 1.

Why?
Inside every computer there is at least one **memory chip**.

A memory chip houses millions of tiny switches, called **transistors**, which store all the computer's information, or **data**.

Transistors can only exist in one of two states:

ON, or **1**, when electricity is flowing through it.

OFF, or **0**, when it isn't.

01101001

A single 1 or 0 is known as a **bit**. A string of bits forms **binary code**, which acts as a set of instructions that tells a computer what to do.

01001000

In binary code, each letter or command typed on a keyboard is converted into a line of eight bits. 'H' is 01001000, and 'i' is 01101001.

Hi

01101001

01001000

H

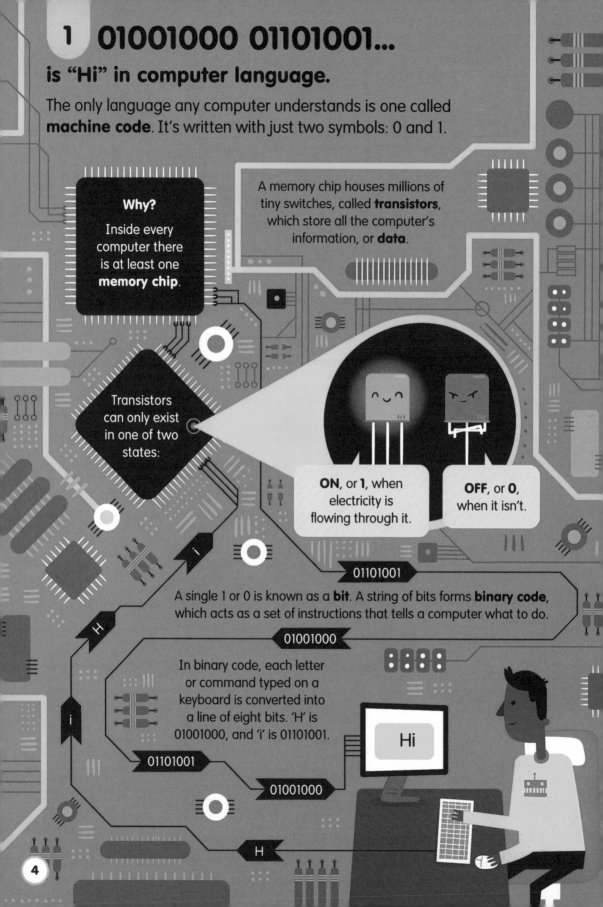

2 To be fluent in computer...

you'd need to learn over 8,000 languages.

Machine code is difficult for humans to read and write, so computer scientists use **programming languages** to write instructions instead. Most coders can write more than one, but nobody understands them all.

A set of instructions is called a **program**. Each language, or **code**, is good for writing some types of programs, but not so good for others.

New languages are created all the time. This page lists just a few by the decade they were written.

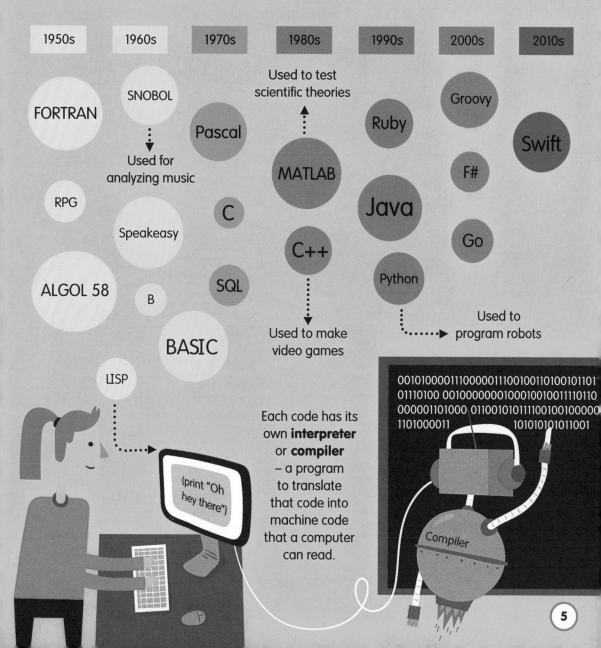

1950s	1960s	1970s	1980s	1990s	2000s	2010s

Used to test scientific theories

SNOBOL

FORTRAN

Groovy

Pascal

Ruby

Swift

Used for analyzing music

MATLAB

F#

RPG

C

Java

Speakeasy

Go

C++

ALGOL 58

SQL

Python

B

Used to program robots

BASIC

Used to make video games

LISP

Each code has its own **interpreter** or **compiler** – a program to translate that code into machine code that a computer can read.

(print "Oh hey there")

0010100001110000011100100110100101101
01110100 001000000010001001001110110
000001101000 0110010101110010010000
1101000011   101010101011001

Compiler

3 The first modern computers...

were a military secret.

In 1946, newspapers around the world reported that a pair of engineers in Philadelphia, USA, had built a new kind of machine called a **computer**. What reporters didn't know was that military spies had already begun using computers during the Second World War...

Daily News

SUNDAY FEBRUARY 15 1946

30-TON ELECTRONIC BRAIN UNVEILED

MEET ENIAC: ELECTRONIC NUMERICAL INTEGRATOR & COMPUTER

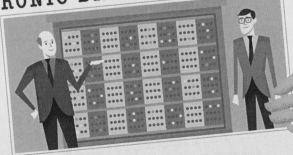

Inventors J. Presper Eckert and John Mauchly, with their team at the University of Pennsylvania, operate their revolutionary machine.

"This mathematical robot works at phenomenal speeds, freeing scientific thought from the drudgery of lengthy calculating work," says ENIAC team.

A computer such as ENIAC is any electronic machine that can:

Store information, usually called data

Follow a set of instructions, called a program, telling it what to do with its data

Display new data, the result of following each program

ENIAC can perform complicated calculations, for example to help figure out exactly where a missile would land after being launched.

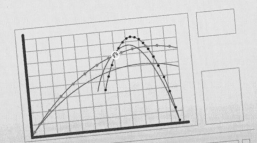

WEDNESDAY JUNE 30 1976

FIRST COMPUTER NOT THE FIRST

In the 1970s, reporters discovered that people had already built and used computers during the Second World War (1939-1945).

In the UK, various versions of a machine called Colossus had been used to crack German codes since 1943. Colossus remained secret after the War, because it was being used to crack Russian codes until 1971.

Design for a Messerschmitt Me 262

In wartime Germany, a machine called Z3, designed in 1941 by engineer Konrad Zuse, was used by aircraft engineers to help with complex calculations. It was destroyed by bombs in 1943. A Z4 model completed in 1944 survived the War, and was later sold to a Swiss company.

A programmer working on a Colossus Mark II machine

4 The invention of the computer...
belongs to everyone.

In 1971, the company that had paid for ENIAC was taken to court for stealing the idea of the computer. A judge found it guilty, but ruled that no single company could own the idea.

The judge declared that the true inventor of the computer was physicist John Atanasoff, who had shared ideas with J. Presper Eckert in 1941.

Most computer historians today credit the key ideas behind how computers work to two mathematicians: John von Neumann and Alan Turing, beginning in the 1930s.

Atanasoff (American)

von Neumann (American-Hungarian)

Turing (British)

5 Most of the internet...

lies underwater.

We think of the internet as a virtual, invisible, imaginary thing, but it's not – it's a *physical* thing. The internet is a huge **network of networks** connecting computers around the world. The networks mostly exist as thousands of miles of cables, deep under the sea.

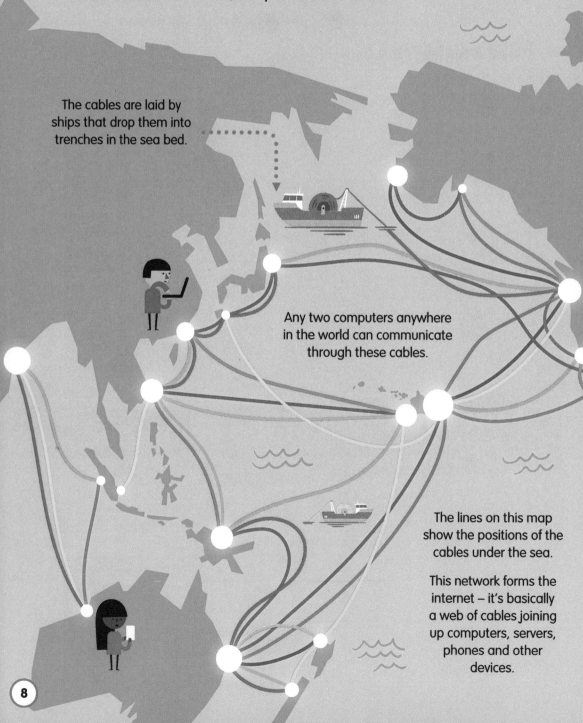

The cables are laid by ships that drop them into trenches in the sea bed.

Any two computers anywhere in the world can communicate through these cables.

The lines on this map show the positions of the cables under the sea.

This network forms the internet – it's basically a web of cables joining up computers, servers, phones and other devices.

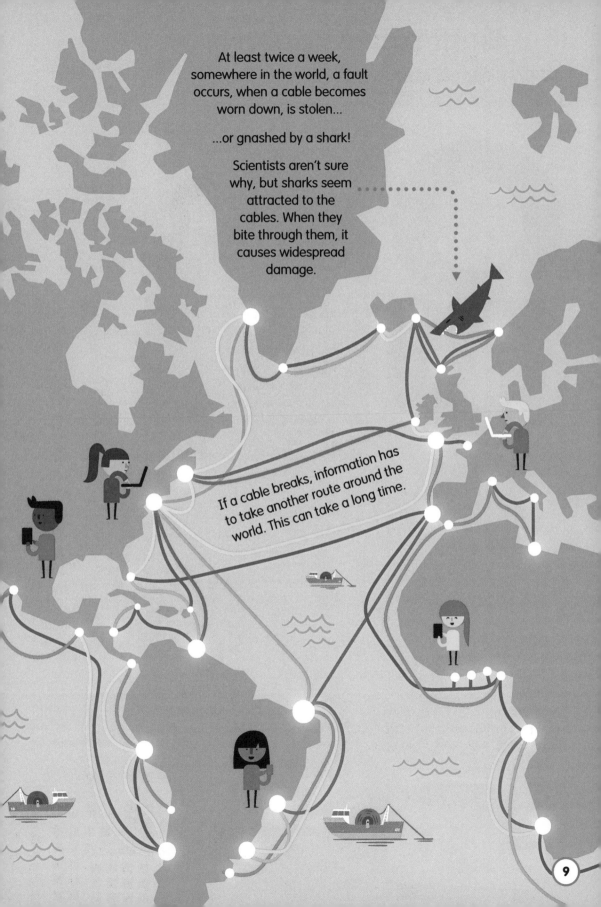

At least twice a week, somewhere in the world, a fault occurs, when a cable becomes worn down, is stolen...

...or gnashed by a shark!

Scientists aren't sure why, but sharks seem attracted to the cables. When they bite through them, it causes widespread damage.

If a cable breaks, information has to take another route around the world. This can take a long time.

The word for 'eight' is written like this in Chinese.

It is pronounced 'ba' in Mandarin, or 'baat' in Cantonese.

'Ba' or 'baat' sound like the words for 'wealth', which are 'fa' in Mandarin or 'faat' in Cantonese. Because of this, eight is thought to be lucky.

On the lucky day of 08/08/2008...

...the Beijing Olympics opened at 8 minutes and 8 seconds past 8.

...a record 300,000 couples registered their marriages in China.

In China and Hong Kong, people spend big sums of money on car license plates containing multiple 8s.

They also pay more for phone numbers with an 8 in them.

Call me on 010-8888888

Apartments on the 8th floor of a building are the most popular.

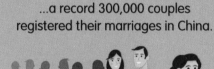

4

The word for 'four' is written like this in Chinese.

It is pronounced 'si' in Mandarin, or 'sei' in Cantonese.

'Si' or 'sei' are pronounced the same as the words for 'death', but with a different pitch. So 4 is believed to be very unlucky.

Tall buildings often don't have a 4th Floor, a 14th Floor or a 24th Floor, because no one would want to live or work there.

7 A dinner party of 13...

was unthinkable in 19th century Paris.

Among some cultures with Christian heritage, 13 is seen as unlucky. So in Paris in the 19th century, dinner party hosts would even pay a stranger to dine with them if it looked likely that the party would be 13 people.

The paid guest was known as the 'quatorizième', which means 'fourteenth' in French.

The Bible describes 13 guests at the final meal that Jesus ate before he was crucified, called the 'Last Supper'. This may be why 13 is considered unlucky.

Time began in 1980...

according to the clocks on GPS satellites.

Global Positioning System technology, or GPS, uses satellites in space. These satellites are fitted with accurate clocks, which have their own particular way of counting time, known as **GPS time**.

GPS time is counted in seconds and weeks, but not days, hours or minutes.

The seconds that pass in a week are counted from 00:00 (midnight) every Sunday. There are 604,800 seconds in a week.

Saturday at 03:00

Sunday at 21:00

0

529,200 · 75,600

SECONDS

453,600 · 151,200

378,000 · 226,800

302,400

Wednesday at 12:00

Scientists set the start time of satellite clocks as midnight on Sunday January 6, 1980.

Every week is given a number. Week zero was January 6-12, 1980.

June 20-26, 1982

0

896 · 128

WEEKS

768 · 256

640 · 384

512

Every 1,024 weeks, which is about 20 years, the week number resets back to zero.

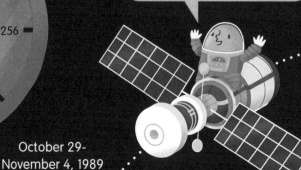

September 25-October 1, 1994

October 29-November 4, 1989

9 Modern clocks...

are based on an Ancient Egyptian system.

The number 12 was hugely important to the people of Ancient Egypt. As well as counting in 12s, they also used it to mark the passing of time.

Egyptian astronomers observed that the Moon had 12 cycles a year.

They also noted 12 stars that rose at regular intervals during the night at certain times of the year. This led them to divide the night into 12 parts.

The earliest-known Egyptian sundials, made 3,500 years ago, divided the day into 12 parts.

During the day, the shadow cast by a rod passed over 12 segments in turn, measuring out each hour.

They made waterclocks with 12 waterlevel marks to show the passing of time by night or day. As water dripped out of a container, it passed a new mark each hour.

The 24-hour clock we use today comes directly from the Egyptian system of splitting night and day into two sets of 12 hours.

10 Two-player computer games...

began with tennis in a laboratory.

In 1958 in Upton, USA, people lined up on the Brookhaven National Laboratory Annual Visitors' Day to play *Tennis for Two*. This was the first ever computer game two opponents could play.

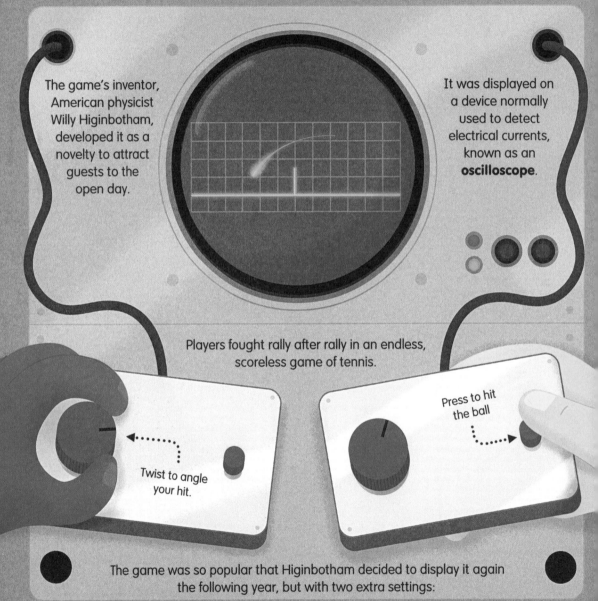

The game's inventor, American physicist Willy Higinbotham, developed it as a novelty to attract guests to the open day.

It was displayed on a device normally used to detect electrical currents, known as an **oscilloscope**.

Players fought rally after rally in an endless, scoreless game of tennis.

Twist to angle your hit.

Press to hit the ball

The game was so popular that Higinbotham decided to display it again the following year, but with two extra settings:

TENNIS ON THE MOON

Players could slow the game down and make the ball lighter, as though they were playing on the Moon, where gravity is weaker...

TENNIS ON JUPITER

...or they could speed it up and make the ball heavier, as if playing tennis on Jupiter, where gravity is stronger.

11 Artificial intelligence...

could be created in two different ways.

One of the hardest challenges in computer science is to create a machine with **artificial intelligence**, that enables it to think and learn in the same way as a human. Some experts believe people are close to conquering this challenge, using two very different methods.

Method 1: hardware

Hardware describes the electronics and physical parts that make up a computer.

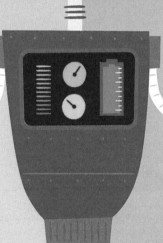

Hardware engineers have already created artificial versions of brain cells.

They've even combined enough of these to mimic some of the connections in an insect brain – but an artificial human brain would require **85 billion** cells.

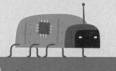

Method 2: software

Software describes the programs that tell computers what to do.

Software engineers are trying to come up with a set of codes that tells computers how to work in a similar way to human brains, but using their own electronic circuits.

The hard part is that no one knows exactly how brains work, so it's not possible to write it into a code.

Be careful what you wish for...

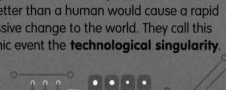

Many computer experts fear that, however it's built, any machine with the power to think and behave better than a human would cause a rapid and massive change to the world. They call this catastrophic event the **technological singularity**.

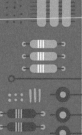

12 More people have the internet...

than access to a flushing toilet.

By 2017 there were:

7.6 **billion** people in the world.

About **6 billion** people with electricity in their homes.

About **3.5 billion** people with access to the internet at home.

Over **5 billion** people with a mobile phone.

Fewer than **3 billion** people with access to a flushing toilet.

In 1995, only **16 million** people had the internet – 0.04% of the population. Now, just over 20 years later, **3.5 billion** have access to it – around 50% of people.

13 Most avalanches occur...

on slopes of 38°.

In winter, snow builds up on the steep slopes of mountains. People can walk or ski safely on these slopes, until the snow reaches an angle of 38°. At that point, it is most likely to tumble down as an avalanche.

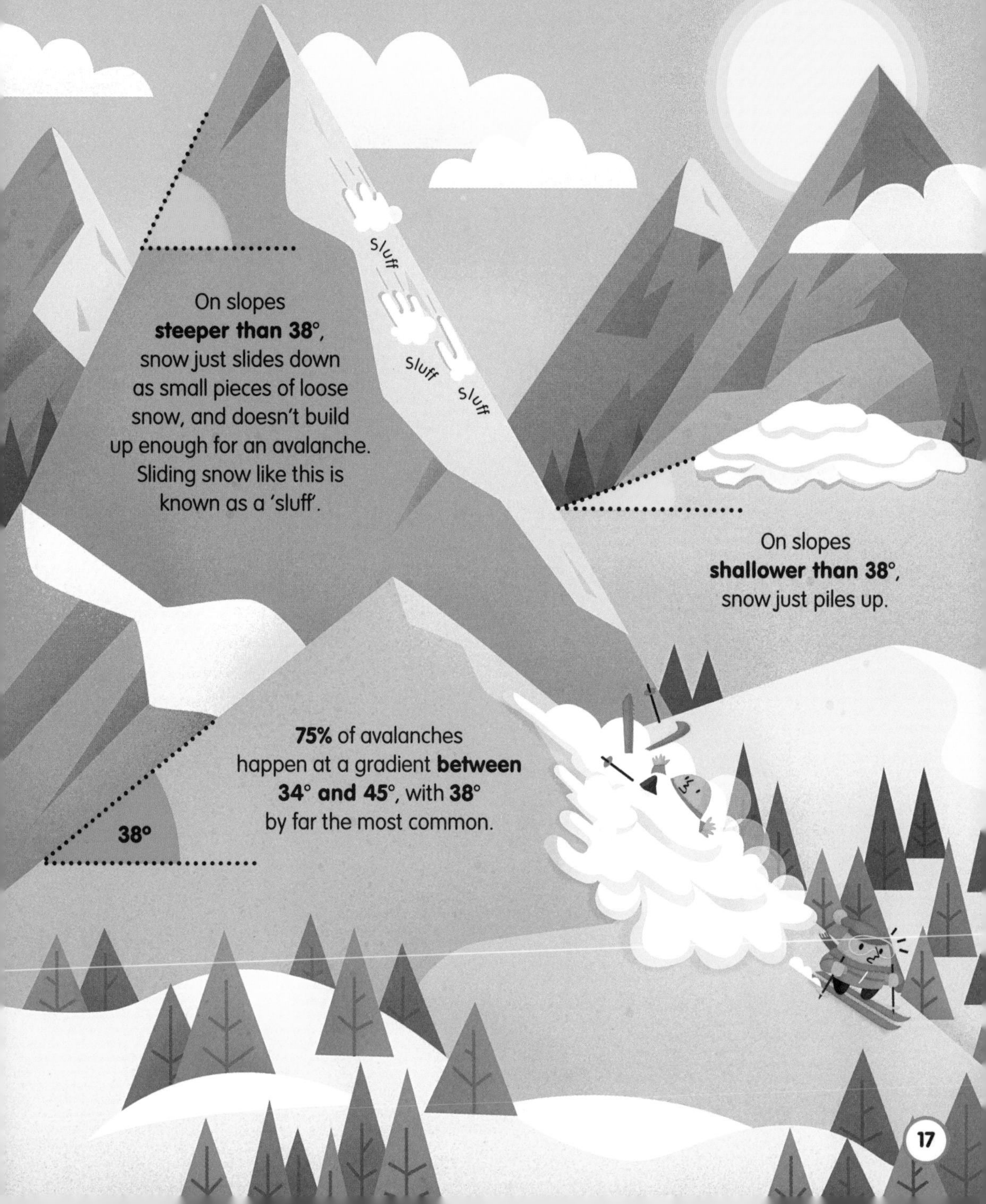

On slopes **steeper than 38°**, snow just slides down as small pieces of loose snow, and doesn't build up enough for an avalanche. Sliding snow like this is known as a 'sluff'.

sluff

sluff *sluff*

On slopes **shallower than 38°**, snow just piles up.

75% of avalanches happen at a gradient **between 34° and 45°**, with **38°** by far the most common.

38°

14 Numbers sent from space...

can pinpoint your location.

Smartphones and GPS navigation devices tell you where you are.
They use signals transmitted by satellites in space to figure it out.

①

Location satellites orbiting the Earth
are constantly sending out signals,
which travel at the speed of light.

②

The signals contain
encoded numbers:

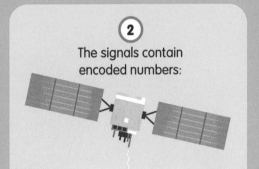

This number
tells the exact
time that the
signal was sent.

These numbers
stand for the exact
location of the
satellite when the
signal was sent.

323827707.004303

26.69, -124.16, 202206.23, 311.3
NW, -12.7, 13 27 44

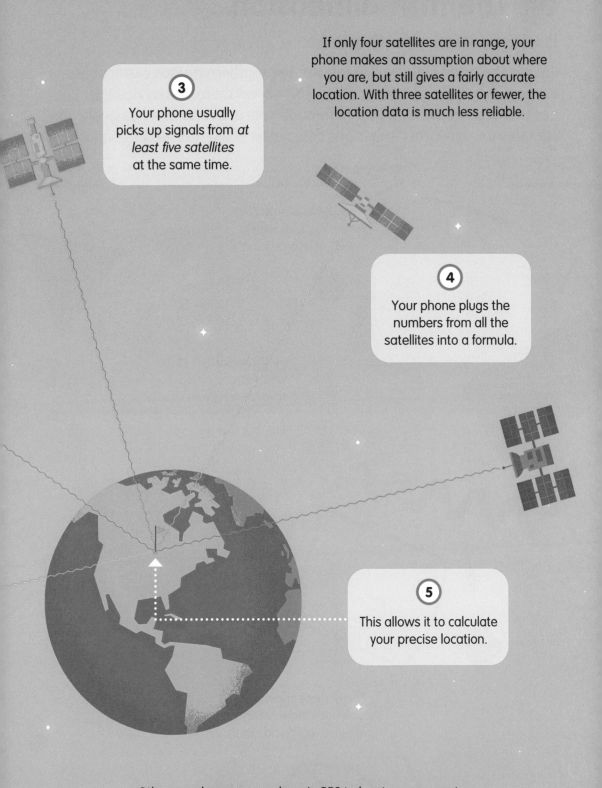

If only four satellites are in range, your phone makes an assumption about where you are, but still gives a fairly accurate location. With three satellites or fewer, the location data is much less reliable.

3
Your phone usually picks up signals from *at least five satellites* at the same time.

4
Your phone plugs the numbers from all the satellites into a formula.

5
This allows it to calculate your precise location.

Other people can use a phone's GPS to locate someone, too. Police sometimes use phones to track criminals or missing people.

15 The fifth dimension...

is closer than you think.

We see the world in three dimensions, but mathematicians commonly use four, five and more dimensions. This allows them to describe the position of an object as it moves through space. But no one has been able to show how five dimensions could exist in the real world – so far...

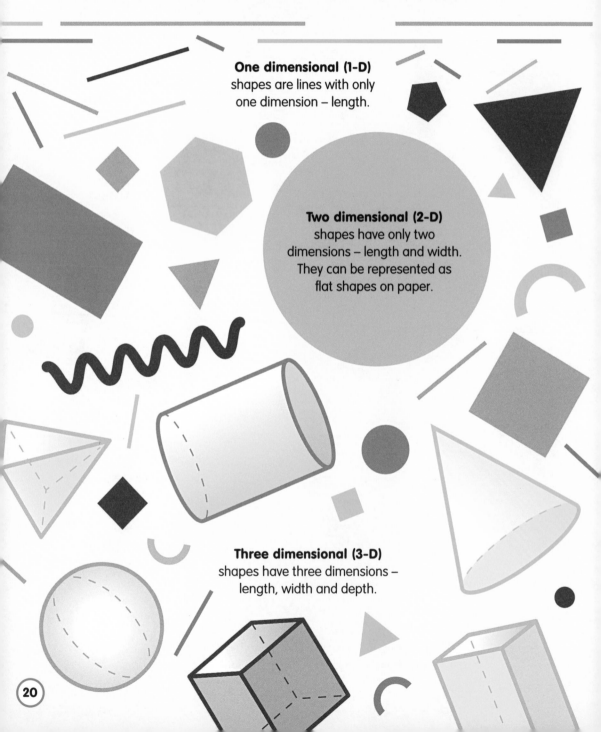

One dimensional (1-D) shapes are lines with only one dimension – length.

Two dimensional (2-D) shapes have only two dimensions – length and width. They can be represented as flat shapes on paper.

Three dimensional (3-D) shapes have three dimensions – length, width and depth.

Scientists think of **time** as another dimension.

They have described 3-D objects moving in a period of time as a way of visualizing **four dimensions**.

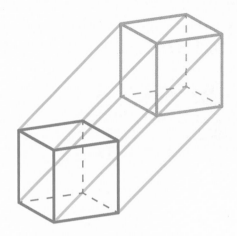

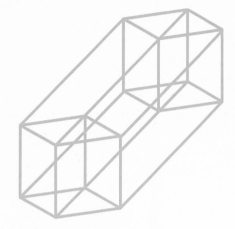

This shows a cube moving through space.

The shape it makes, called a **tesseract**, represents a 4-D cube.

No one has been able to make sense of a **fifth dimension**, although equations with five dimensions are common in mathematics.

Scientists studying a branch of physics known as **string theory** think the universe might have more than five dimensions. If these exist, they would alter the behavior of ripples of energy in space, called **gravitational waves**.

Gravitational waves were detected for the first time in 2015...

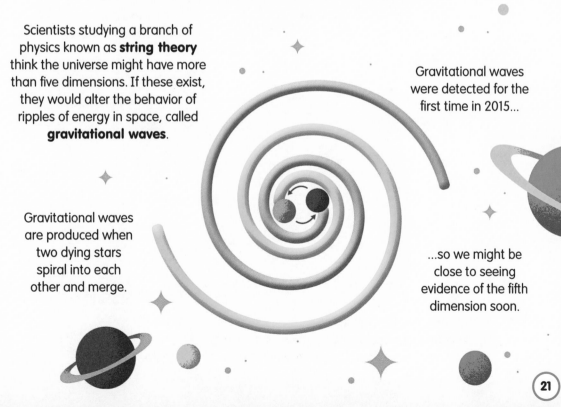

Gravitational waves are produced when two dying stars spiral into each other and merge.

...so we might be close to seeing evidence of the fifth dimension soon.

16 If R_e is greater than one...

an outbreak is getting worse.

When a disease infects more people in a community than disease experts expect, they call it an **outbreak**. They calculate a value known as the **effective reproductive number**, or **Re**, to track whether the outbreak is growing or dying. This helps them work out how to bring it under control.

Imagine a class of 20 students in which 2 students catch a virus. None of the other students are immune.

⋯⋯⋯▶

One week later, 4 students have caught the virus from the first 2.

Newly infected students

$$R_e = 4 \div 2 = 2$$

Previously infected students

R_e is the average number of *new people* an infected person goes on to infect. So, in this case...

If R_e is greater than one, it means the outbreak is getting worse.

If it's less than one, the outbreak is dying down.

A substance that makes you immune to a disease is called a **vaccine**. By studying the numbers of people affected, health officials know when to use vaccines to prevent outbreaks.

17 Viral videos spread faster...

than viral diseases.

A **viral video** is any clip or animation that rapidly gains views through being shared online. They are referred to as 'viral' because each time they're shared, they reach new people – like viruses that spread diseases.

Below are some of the fastest spreading viral videos, based on the number of views generated in just 24 hours.

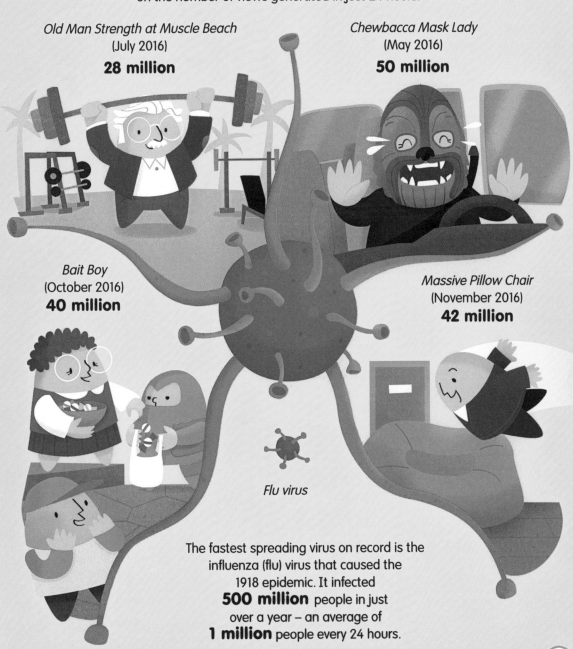

Old Man Strength at Muscle Beach
(July 2016)
28 million

Chewbacca Mask Lady
(May 2016)
50 million

Bait Boy
(October 2016)
40 million

Massive Pillow Chair
(November 2016)
42 million

Flu virus

The fastest spreading virus on record is the influenza (flu) virus that caused the 1918 epidemic. It infected **500 million** people in just over a year – an average of **1 million** people every 24 hours.

In an emergency, dial 911...

Or 999. Or 112. Or 1515...

Emergency phone numbers are usually short and memorable.
Similar phone numbers are used all over the world.

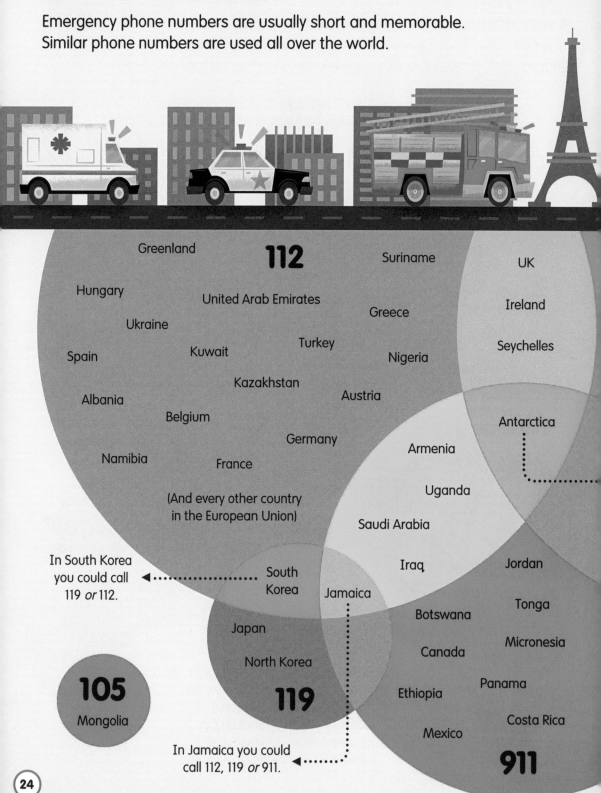

112

Greenland
Suriname
UK

Hungary
United Arab Emirates
Ireland

Greece

Ukraine
Seychelles

Turkey

Spain
Kuwait
Nigeria

Kazakhstan

Albania
Austria

Belgium

Antarctica

Germany
Armenia

Namibia
France
Uganda

(And every other country
in the European Union)
Saudi Arabia

In South Korea
you could call
119 *or* 112.
South
Korea
Jamaica
Iraq
Jordan

Tonga
Botswana

Japan
Canada
Micronesia

North Korea

105
119
Ethiopia
Panama

Mongolia
Costa Rica

Mexico

In Jamaica you could
call 112, 119 *or* 911.
911

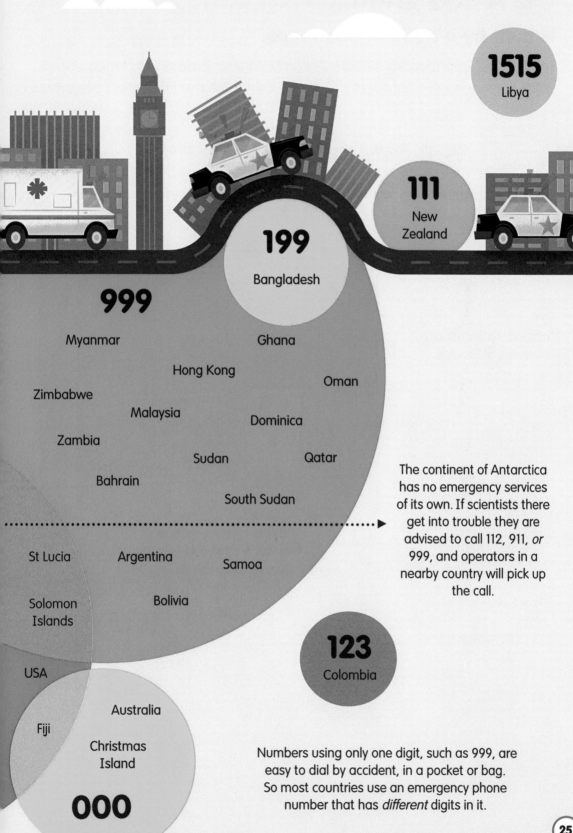

1515
Libya

111
New Zealand

199
Bangladesh

999

Myanmar

Ghana

Hong Kong

Oman

Zimbabwe

Malaysia

Dominica

Zambia

Sudan

Qatar

Bahrain

South Sudan

The continent of Antarctica has no emergency services of its own. If scientists there get into trouble they are advised to call 112, 911, *or* 999, and operators in a nearby country will pick up the call.

St Lucia

Argentina

Samoa

Solomon Islands

Bolivia

USA

123
Colombia

Australia

Fiji

Christmas Island

000

Numbers using only one digit, such as 999, are easy to dial by accident, in a pocket or bag. So most countries use an emergency phone number that has *different* digits in it.

19 A sea shell...

is built by a number sequence.

The spiral shape of many sea shells can be drawn from an arrangement of squares, made from numbers in a series known as the **Fibonacci sequence**.

This is the Fibonacci sequence: **1, 1, 2, 3, 5, 8, 13, 21, 34, 55**

The next number in the sequence is found by adding up the two numbers before it.
$1 + 1 = 2$ $1 + 2 = 3$ $2 + 3 = 5$ $3 + 5 = 8$ $5 + 8 = 13$

Imagine the sequence as a series of squares...

The length of the side of each new square is the same as the sides of the two previous squares added together.

This spiral is created by drawing a curve connecting two opposite corners of each square.

The Fibonacci sequence appears throughout nature, in shells, animal horns and the spiral pattern of seeds in sunflowers, pine cones and pineapples.

The scales on a pineapple form diagonal spirals – this one has 8 in one direction, and 13 in the other.

A similar pattern is found on pine cones. The numbers 8 and 13 are consecutive Fibonacci numbers.

20 The Encyclopedia of Sequences...

has more than 300,000 entries.

To mathematicians, the word *sequence* means something very specific: a series of numbers, in a particular order, that follows a rule that describes how to get from one number to the next. Every time someone finds a new sequence, it is submitted to the Encyclopedia, checked and registered.

The Encyclopedia of Sequences only covers whole numbers, known as **integers**. Sequence **A000027** describes the basic integer sequence:

1, 2, 3, 4, 5, 6, 7, 8, 9, 10...

Every sequence accepted by the Encyclopedia is given a unique entry number. Not all are to do with pure mathematics. **A145330** lists the numbers to press on a phone keypad to play the theme music from *Star Wars*:

1, 5, 4, 3, 2, 8, 5, 4, 3, 2, 8, 5, 4, 3, 4, 2

A116448 lists the number of days in a year on each of the planets in our solar system:

88, 225, 365, 687, 4333, 10756, 30707, 60223

One famous sequence has troubled mathematicians for centuries – the sequence of **prime numbers**. (Entry **A000040**). These are numbers that can only be divided by themselves and 1, but no other whole number.

2, 3, 5, 7, 11, 13, 17, 19, 23...

Finding a pattern that explains how to get from one prime number to the next is one of the greatest unsolved problems of mathematics.

21 Numbers don't exist...

or do they?

People have been arguing for centuries over whether numbers really exist...

Some philosophers said that if you can't see or touch numbers, then they don't exist. They were later known as **nominalists**.

> You can hold two apples... but you can't hold the number two.

A Greek thinker named **Plato** believed that objects exist in the physical world...

> ...but numbers exist in a kind of abstract heaven, beyond time and space.

3320

5583

11

2

Plato's heaven

356   567

49   99967

Physical world

Apples

Vase   Flower   **Plato**   Building

Aristotle, Plato's pupil, argued that numbers only exist as abstract ideas in our minds.

888   9
4
31   19
7262

> So without human minds to think about them, numbers disappear.

But later philosophers and scientists came up with a different idea...

> Numbers also describe things such as the speed of a falling object. Objects still fall even if people aren't there to see them.

gravity = 9.8m/s²

time = 2s   velocity = gt

velocity = 19.6m/s

> Therefore numbers *do* exist...

22 "I'm the Creeper...

catch me if you can" – said the first computer virus.

Computer viruses are programs that a creator uploads onto another person's computer without permission. Nowadays, most viruses are designed to cause harm, but the first were experimental programs designed to test out new kinds of computer code.

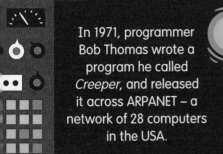

In 1971, programmer Bob Thomas wrote a program he called *Creeper*, and released it across ARPANET – a network of 28 computers in the USA.

To prove *Creeper* had found a new computer, it left a message...

Thomas wanted to see if he could make *Creeper* jump from one computer to another. This type of virus is known today as a **worm**.

23 Light...

could power super-fast computers.

Inside computers, data travels through copper wires as a stream of tiny particles called **electrons**. But scientists are experimenting with ways to send data between electronic chips using *light*, which carries far more information.

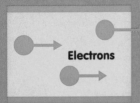

Copper wire

Electrons

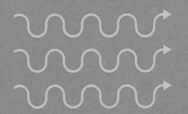

Photons

Light source

Currently, data carried by electrons through wires moves at about half the speed of light or slower.

Light is made of tiny particles, called **photons**. Unlike electrons, photons have no mass and face no resistance as they travel.

Light photons carry **20** times more information than electrons. They use far less energy and can move at *almost* the speed of light through air.

I'M THE CREEPER. CATCH ME IF YOU CAN.

...on the screen saying...

In response, programmer Ray Tomlinson wrote *Reaper*, an **anti-virus** program that could also jump between computers. Whenever *Reaper* found the *Creeper* code, it deleted it.

Here's an impression of the design scientists are developing:

Photon switch

Cable

Chip

Tiny switches would bend the light, enabling it to turn corners.

Hollow glass threads

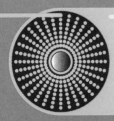

Cable

Inside the cable, data would travel at high speed through air inside hollow glass threads.

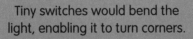

Computers mix three colors...

in over sixteen million combinations.

A computer monitor is made up of tiny squares, called **pixels**, which together build up images. Computers mix colors to fill each pixel. The total number of combinations is greater than the number of colors most humans can see.

To fill pixels, computers use a palette made up of

3 colors

Red · Green · Blue

Each of these has

256 shades

The total number of ways these shades can be combined is 256 x 256 x 256, which comes to...

16,777,216

Biologists estimate that humans can typically make out **10,000,000** different colors.

This means neighboring pixels can be filled with slightly different combinations that the human eye can't tell apart.

No combination ever appears as a blank spot. Instead, the brain interprets similar combinations as the same shade.

25 Some numbers become letters...

in scientific calculations.

Some numbers represent important scientific values – such as the speed of light – and are used over and over again in different calculations. So to save time and effort, scientists use single letters to represent them.

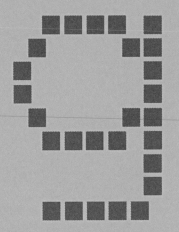

The letter **g** represents **gravity at the surface of the Earth** – the force that pulls objects to the ground as they fall. It is measured in meters (or feet) per second per second.

$$g = 9.8m/s^2 \ (32ft/s^2)$$

For any circle, the length of its perimeter divided by its diameter always comes to the same number:
3.14159265358979323846...

The digits go on and on without a pattern. It can't be written as a simple fraction either, so it is written as π or **pi** instead. Pi is the first letter of the Greek word *periphereia*, meaning perimeter.

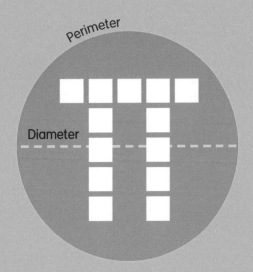

Perimeter

Diameter

The letter **c** represents the **speed of light**.

It stands for *celeritas*, the word for speed in Latin.

$$c = 299{,}792{,}458m/s \ (983{,}571{,}056ft/s)$$

26 Fuzzy logic...

cooks fluffy rice.

Fuzzy logic is a form of coding that helps computers make decisions more like humans. It is used to predict earthquakes and run entire subway systems, but can also teach a machine to cook the perfect bowl of rice.

Ordinary computers use a built-in logic, called binary logic, that thinks solely in terms of 'yes' and 'no'. Early electric rice cookers ran on this type of logic too.

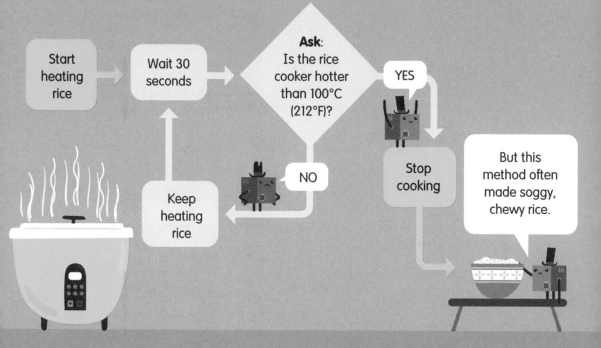

Start heating rice → Wait 30 seconds → **Ask:** Is the rice cooker hotter than 100°C (212°F)?

YES → Stop cooking

NO → Keep heating rice

But this method often made soggy, chewy rice.

The manufacturers realized that not every question can be answered with a binary 'yes' or 'no' – there are 'fuzzy' answers in between, such as 'almost', 'slightly' or 'very'.

So they programmed a model using fuzzy logic instead.

Fuzzy logic takes the answers in between into account.

RICE

WATER

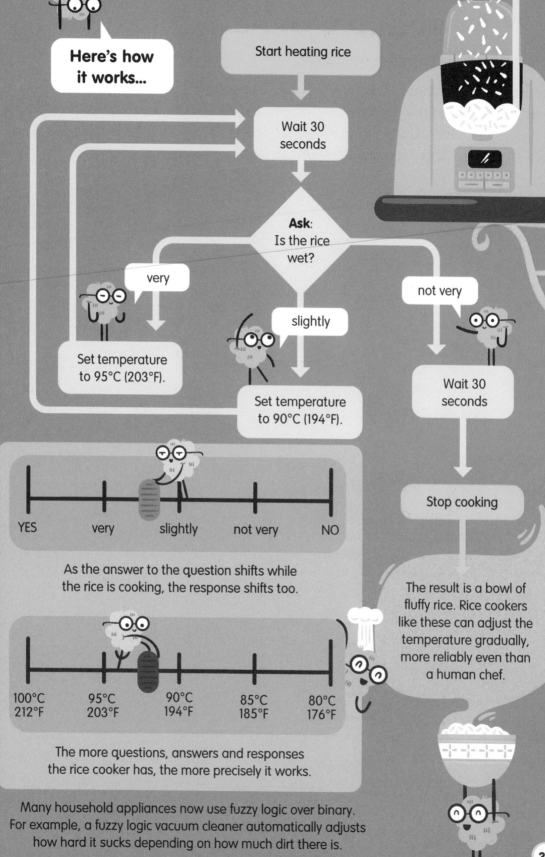

Here's how it works...

Start heating rice

Wait 30 seconds

Ask: Is the rice wet?

very

slightly

not very

Set temperature to 95°C (203°F).

Set temperature to 90°C (194°F).

Wait 30 seconds

Stop cooking

| YES | very | slightly | not very | NO |

As the answer to the question shifts while the rice is cooking, the response shifts too.

| 100°C 212°F | 95°C 203°F | 90°C 194°F | 85°C 185°F | 80°C 176°F |

The more questions, answers and responses the rice cooker has, the more precisely it works.

The result is a bowl of fluffy rice. Rice cookers like these can adjust the temperature gradually, more reliably even than a human chef.

Many household appliances now use fuzzy logic over binary. For example, a fuzzy logic vacuum cleaner automatically adjusts how hard it sucks depending on how much dirt there is.

35

27 Microchip graffiti...

was used to prevent theft.

Microchips, or **chips**, are tiny electronic components that process and store all the information inside a computer. Chip manufacturers used to etch images into their chips to prove that they'd made them, and stop others from stealing their designs. This was known as **microchip graffiti**.

Their graffiti, also called **silicon doodles**, took many different forms. Here are some examples.

The designs were hidden among the electrical circuits and switches that made up the rest of the chip.

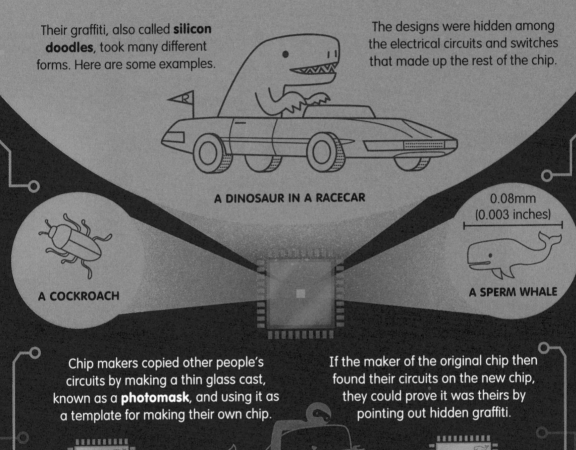

A DINOSAUR IN A RACECAR

A COCKROACH

0.08mm
(0.003 inches)

A SPERM WHALE

Chip makers copied other people's circuits by making a thin glass cast, known as a **photomask**, and using it as a template for making their own chip.

If the maker of the original chip then found their circuits on the new chip, they could prove it was theirs by pointing out hidden graffiti.

Nowadays, microchip graffiti is a dying art, for various reasons.

THE LAW

Laws have been introduced across the world that make it illegal to copy chips. There's less need for graffiti because theft has since died down

TINY ERRORS

In a few rare cases, doodles were misplaced by a matter of micrometers, damaging the circuitry. This caused chip companies to tighten their rules

All numbers can be made from...

triangles and squares.

Mathematicians have always been fascinated by numbers that can be arranged into regular shapes. For example, triangular and square numbers. Over the centuries, they have searched for links between the sequences these numbers make.

Triangular numbers	**Square numbers**

1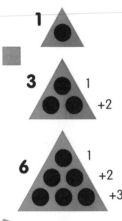

3 1 +2

6 1 +2 +3

10 1 +2 +3 +4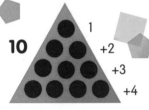

15 1 +2 +3 +4 +5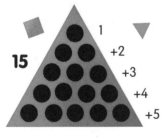

In 1638, **Pierre de Fermat** said he could make any number by adding three (or fewer) triangular numbers, or four (or fewer) square numbers, or five (or fewer) pentagon numbers, and so on. This works for all regular-sided shapes.

For example, 31 can be made by 3 triangular numbers (15 + 10 + 6), or 4 square numbers (25 + 4 + 1 + 1).

1

4 (2 x 2)

9 (3 x 3)

16 (4 x 4)

25 (5 x 5)

The next, or 6th, number in this sequence is 1 + 2 + 3 + 4 + 5 + 6 = 21.

The next, or 6th, number in this sequence is 6 x 6 = 36.

For centuries, mathematicians struggled to prove Fermat's idea. In 1813, **Augustin-Louis Cauchy** finally proved it worked for all numbers and regular shapes.

29 Prime numbers...

help insects survive.

Insects called cicadas spend most of their lives buried underground. Some species, called periodical cicadas, only emerge every 13 or 17 years.
The numbers 13 and 17 are **prime numbers** – that is, numbers that are divisible only by one or themselves – and that turns out to be very important...

Populations of animals tend to go up and down at regular intervals, over time. These fluctuations are known as **population cycles**.

A cicada can stay out of harm's way by only having a *high* population in years when its predators have a *low* population.

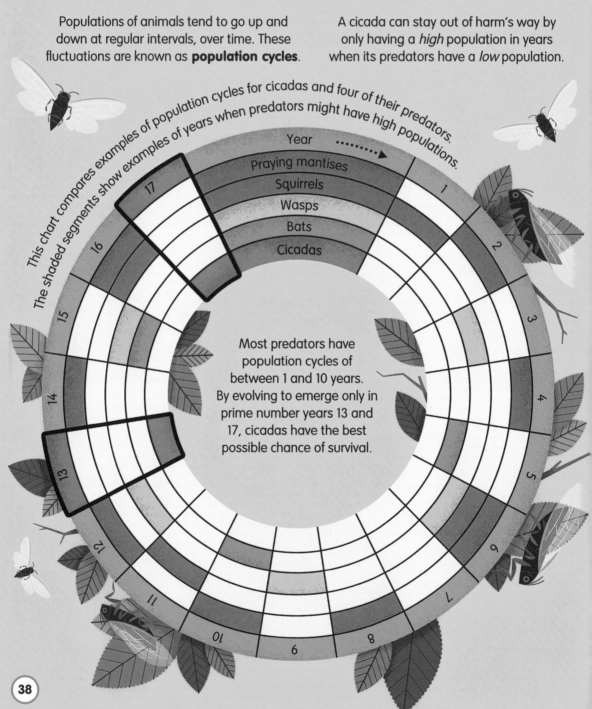

This chart compares examples of population cycles for cicadas and four of their predators. The shaded segments show examples of years when predators might have high populations.

Year

Praying mantises
Squirrels
Wasps
Bats
Cicadas

Most predators have population cycles of between 1 and 10 years. By evolving to emerge only in prime number years 13 and 17, cicadas have the best possible chance of survival.

1 2 3 4 5 6 7 8 9 10 11 12 13 14 15 16 17

30 An international internet crash...
was caused by a garden tool.

Cables that stretch from the Black Sea through Georgia to Armenia and Azerbaijan provide all three countries with the internet. These cables mostly run underground, but can become exposed by landslides or heavy rain.

The Black Sea

Underground internet cable

In 2011, Aishtan Shakarian, a 75-year-old woman in Georgia, was digging for copper to sell as scrap metal.

Georgia

As she dug, she pierced an internet cable that was buried beneath a field.

Azerbaijan

Cable to Azerbaijan

Cable to Armenia

Armenia

Across Armenia, Azerbaijan and parts of Georgia, over **3 million** people lost internet access.

Her slip-up left Armenia's internet service down for almost half a day. This might not sound like very long, but Armenia's population of **2.9 million** relied on the internet for many vital things, such as...

...making credit card payments...

...broadcasting news...

No medical records available

...and accessing crucial information.

31 An island's coastline...

is impossible to measure exactly.

Coasts are full of inlets, cracks, fissures and bays, which makes them impossible to measure exactly. The measurement you get varies wildly depending on how much detail you go into when measuring it, as this map of mainland Britain shows.

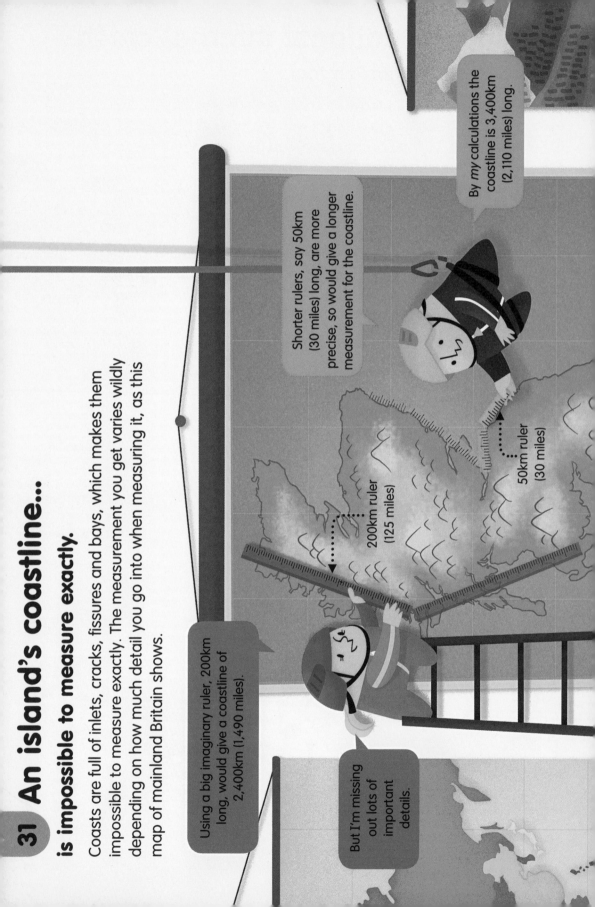

By *my* calculations the coastline is 3,400km (2,110 miles) long.

Shorter rulers, say 50km (30 miles) long, are more precise, so would give a longer measurement for the coastline.

50km ruler (30 miles)

200km ruler (125 miles)

Using a big imaginary ruler, 200km long, would give a coastline of 2,400km (1,490 miles).

But I'm missing out lots of important details.

32 Scientists risked their lives...

to measure a meter.

In 18th-century Europe, a wide range of measurements was used for length. French scientists set out to find a new unit, the **meter**, that could be easily divided by 10 or 100. But France was in turmoil after the French Revolution in 1789, so setting a meter's *exact* length proved dangerous.

North Pole

In 1791, French scientists set the distance from the North Pole to the Equator as 10 million meters.

10 million meters

Dunkirk

1 million meters

Barcelona

The following year, expert surveyors set out to measure a tenth of this distance, a section of land from Dunkirk in France, to Barcelona in Spain. By dividing this length by 1 million, they could find the length of 1 meter.

But in France, anyone suspected of being against the Revolution was in danger of execution. The surveyors were temporarily arrested, suspected of being supporters of the old regime.

Equator

At that time, Spain was at war with France. In Spain, the surveyors were arrested and imprisoned on suspicion of being French spies. In 1793, the meter was officially set – but not for good...

33 The speed of light...

defines the length of a meter.

The official definition of a meter has changed three times
since it was first introduced in 1793.

1793: 1 meter was set to be $\dfrac{1}{10,000,000}$ the distance from the North Pole to the Equator.

1799: 1 meter was redefined as the length of a specific metal bar (created in France).

1889: a new bar was cast from platinum and iridium, and
thirty copies were made and sent to different countries.

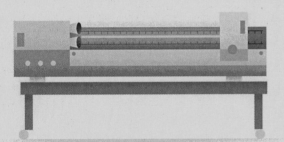

But, viewed under a microscope, there were very
slight differences in length between each bar.

1960: 1 meter was redefined again, as
1,650,763.73 wavelengths of light emitted
by a gas known as krypton-86. But even
these wavelengths vary by tiny amounts.

1983:

Scientists used a measurement that never changes: the speed
of light. This is always 299,792,458m per second.
A meter is now defined as:

the distance light travels in $\dfrac{1}{299,792,458}$ of a second.

The first computer bugs...

really were insects.

Computer programmers today use the word 'bug' to describe problems with the code that tells computers what to do. But the term first came into common use when a programmer had trouble with moths.

In 1947, a US naval officer named **Grace Hopper** was programming a computer called the **Harvard Mark II**.

In the 1940s, computers were so large they filled whole rooms. The heat they generated attracted all sorts of insects, which regularly caused problems.

A moth was discovered stuck in a switch in the Harvard Mark II, stopping it from working.

The moth was removed and attached to Hopper's written log. This gave rise to the term 'debugging' – meaning fixing problems – which has been in popular use ever since.

35 Different kilograms...

weigh different amounts.

All metric weights are based on the original kilogram, a small cylinder of platinum and iridium metal known as **Big K** created in 1879. Although it is used as the official international standard, it seems to be getting lighter...

A kilogram is defined as the weight of Big K, whatever the weight of Big K might be.

Exact copies of Big K exist. But they no longer weigh the same as the original Big K. Either *they're* getting heavier, or *it's* getting lighter.

A — Big K is kept inside a bell jar...

B — ...inside another bell jar...

C — ...locked in a vacuum chamber in Paris.

Occasional cleaning may have wiped microscopic particles away – or the copies may be getting heavier as air molecules stick to them. No one is sure.

Le Grand K
(French for Big K)

Scientists have now agreed to set a new international standard for the kilogram, that doesn't depend on a single object. This standard is based on constant values, including the speed of light, and the movement of energy inside certain atoms.

36 A software glitch...
let thousands of prisoners out of jail early.

In 2002, in the state of Washington, USA, some software designed to calculate prisoners' release dates was programmed incorrectly. As a result, 3,200 prisoners were released early.

Software errors, often called glitches, can be the result of a single misplaced letter or symbol.

Here are some other outcomes of software errors.

ROCKET EXPLOSION

In the USA in 1962, a piece of software was written to launch an unmanned rocket into space. But the wrong kind of hyphen was written into the code.

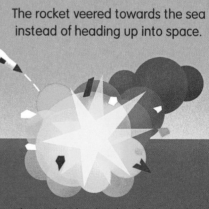

The rocket veered towards the sea instead of heading up into space.

The rocket had to be destroyed in a controlled explosion to avoid it crashing into some ships.

WORLD WAR III NEAR MISS

In 1983, the Soviet Union and the USA were on the brink of war. The Soviet Union built a computer system which could spot any missiles launched against them, from a long way off.

One day, the computer system triggered a warning that the USA had attacked. But the software had actually mistaken unusual light conditions for a missile.

WARNING!

Thankfully, a military commander mistrusted the computer and decided not to retaliate, so a potential war was avoided.

LIVING PATIENTS DECLARED DEAD

In 2003, a hospital in Michigan, USA, updated its software for managing patient records.

But there was a mistake in the update and 8,500 living patients were declared dead.

The hospital had to quickly fix the mistake because 'dead' patients aren't eligible for medical treatment.

B-but, I'm not dead!

I know they sometimes cause trouble, but personally I'm a fan of software glitches.

DEAD

Some numbers are so big...

they become a symbol.

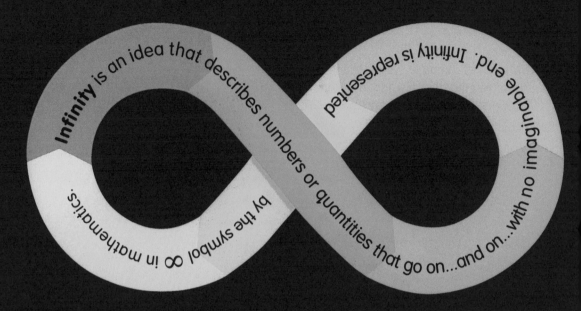

Infinity is an idea that describes numbers or quantities that go on...and on...with no imaginable end. Infinity is represented by the symbol ∞ in mathematics.

38 One divided by infinity...

is practically zero.

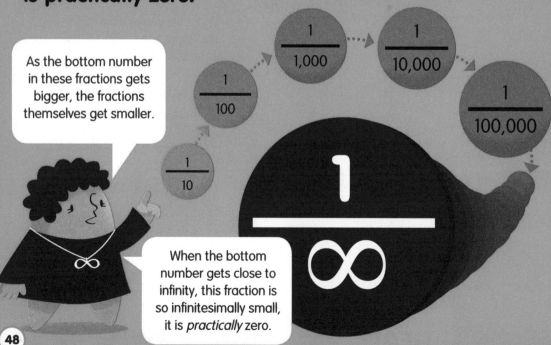

As the bottom number in these fractions gets bigger, the fractions themselves get smaller.

$$\frac{1}{10}$$

$$\frac{1}{100}$$

$$\frac{1}{1,000}$$

$$\frac{1}{10,000}$$

$$\frac{1}{100,000}$$

$$\frac{1}{\infty}$$

When the bottom number gets close to infinity, this fraction is so infinitesimally small, it is *practically* zero.

39 Infinity...

is a paradox.

For centuries, mathematicians struggled to define infinity, because it led to contradictions, known as **paradoxes**. Here's an example to show how one infinity that appears bigger than another, is in fact the same size.

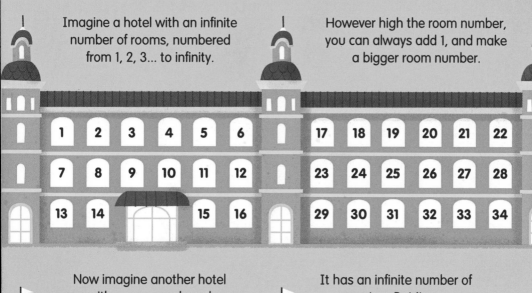

Imagine a hotel with an infinite number of rooms, numbered from 1, 2, 3... to infinity.

However high the room number, you can always add 1, and make a bigger room number.

Now imagine another hotel with rooms numbered from 2, 4, 6... to infinity.

It has an infinite number of rooms, too. But its rooms only have even numbers.

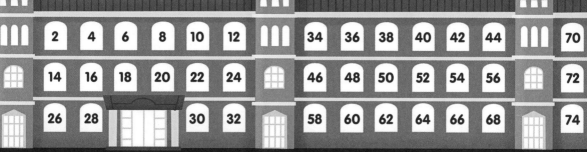

The paradox

The orange hotel *appears* to have more rooms than the blue hotel, because its rooms are numbered with all the even numbers *and* all the odd numbers.

But every room in the orange hotel can be matched to a room in the blue hotel by multiplying its number by 2.

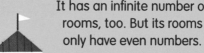

1	....	2
2	....	4
3	....	6
4	....	8
5	....	10

Therefore, the hotels are the same size.

40 Sharing pictures...

creates jigsaw puzzles for your computer.

Files, such as pictures, are often too large to travel through the internet in one big piece. Instead, they are broken up into smaller pieces called **packets**. Packets are sent individually across the cables that make up the internet, and put back together at the other end.

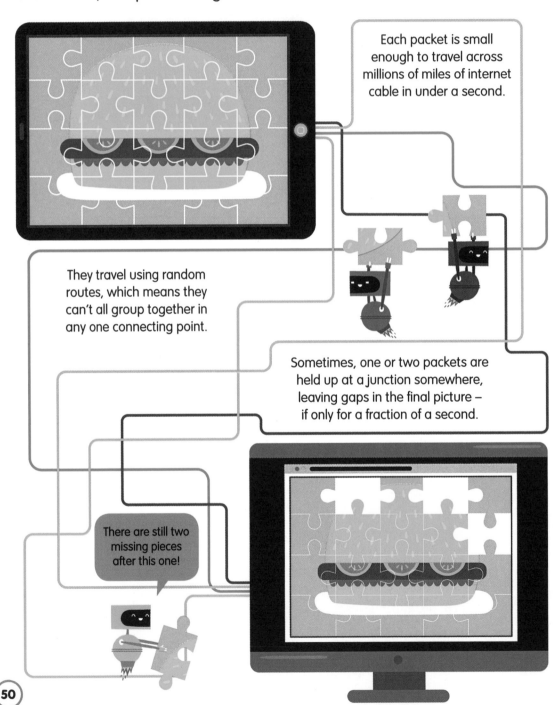

Each packet is small enough to travel across millions of miles of internet cable in under a second.

They travel using random routes, which means they can't all group together in any one connecting point.

Sometimes, one or two packets are held up at a junction somewhere, leaving gaps in the final picture – if only for a fraction of a second.

There are still two missing pieces after this one!

41 A champion mathlete...

can add ten ten-digit numbers in thirteen seconds.

Every two years, a Mental Calculation World Cup takes place in Germany. The competitors, sometimes known as **mathletes**, solve complicated calculations incredibly quickly, all in their heads.

Rules of the World Cup:

No calculators allowed

Complete silence during the competition

Workings on paper not permitted

Here are some of the challenges from the 2016 Mental Calculation World Cup:

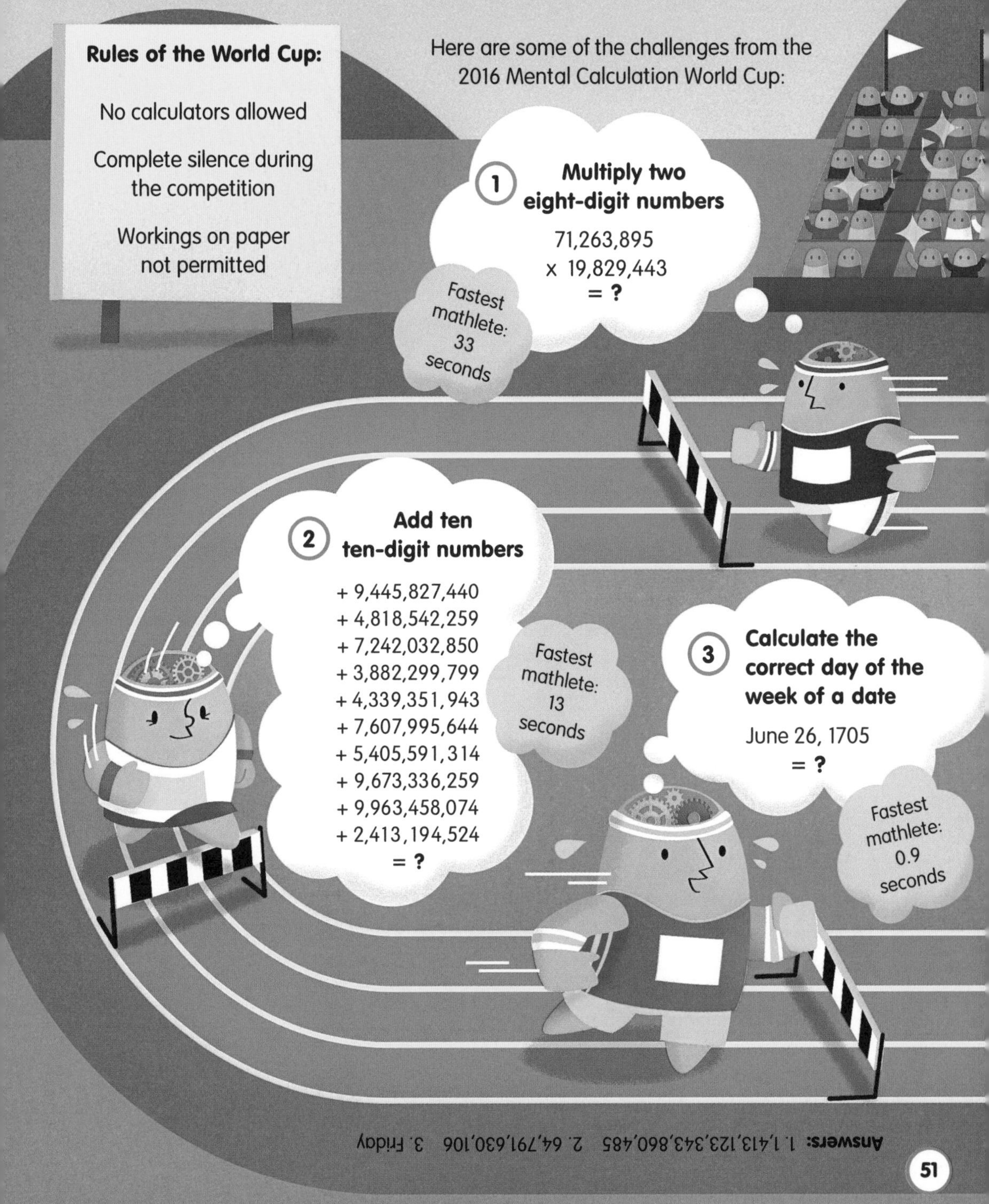

1 Multiply two eight-digit numbers

71,263,895
x 19,829,443
= ?

Fastest mathlete: 33 seconds

2 Add ten ten-digit numbers

+ 9,445,827,440
+ 4,818,542,259
+ 7,242,032,850
+ 3,882,299,799
+ 4,339,351,943
+ 7,607,995,644
+ 5,405,591,314
+ 9,673,336,259
+ 9,963,458,074
+ 2,413,194,524
= ?

Fastest mathlete: 13 seconds

3 Calculate the correct day of the week of a date

June 26, 1705
= ?

Fastest mathlete: 0.9 seconds

Answers: 1. 1,413,123,343,860,485 2. 64,791,630,106 3. Friday

42 Zero came after one...

in the history of counting.

Subtracting a number from itself gives **zero**, the number that represents nothing. But zero hasn't always existed – people invented it long after they began counting and carrying out mathematical calculations.

Babylon, 2,300 years ago

Before zero was defined as the number that comes before one, Babylonians put zeros in the middle of bigger numbers – much like the zero in 3,603 that indicates a lack of tens.

The Babylonian symbol for zero

India, 7th century

Astronomer **Brahmagupta** invented rules for a number called *shunya*, the Sanskrit word for 'empty'.

Shunya followed similar rules to modern day zero.

$$1 + shunya = 1$$

$$1 - shunya = 1$$

$$1 \times shunya = shunya$$

Shunya was different from the Babylonian zero. It was a number on its own, not just part of larger numbers.

Baghdad, 9th century

Mathematician **Muhammed ibn Musa al-Khwarizmi** translated Brahmagupta's works into Arabic, and adopted his rules for *shunya*.

His symbol for zero was a dot. ⋯⋯▶ ●

Since then, many different symbols have been used.

43 Banning numbers...

inspired a secret code.

Europeans didn't have a number for *nothing* until the Middle Ages. Then they came into contact with Arabs from North Africa and the Middle East, who introduced them to a way of counting that included zero. Many Europeans greeted it with suspicion, but others used it to keep secrets...

Late 1100s: Italian mathematician **Leonardo Fibonacci** learned the Arabic system when he studied calculation in Algeria in his youth.

1202: Fibonacci published *Liber Abaci*, in which he showed the practical uses of Arabic numbers in banking and trade.

1299: The Italian city of Florence banned bankers and merchants from using Arabic numbers.

The authorities believed Arabic numbers encouraged fraud – zero could easily be changed into a six or a nine.

You owe the bank 190 soldi

But merchants found that calculations using Arabic numbers were much quicker than other methods...

...so they continued to use them in secret, by writing coded messages.

Some historians claim they named their code after the Arabic word for zero, *sifr*...

...which later evolved into **cipher**, a word for code that's still used today.

44 Databases of facial expressions...

enable computers to see.

Computer vision is a science that aims to give computers the ability to interpret an image or video. To do this, computers compare what's on their screen, or what's in front of them, to millions of photographs and videos in online databases, then decide what they think they can 'see'.

They search thousands of different databases that cover as wide a range of images as possible, such as...

Flowers

Facial expressions

Cats

But computers don't get it right every time. They can only recognize situations that look similar to what's included in the databases, so some images confuse them. A computer might think that...

AN ADULT IN A WIG SINGING KARAOKE

...is in fact...

A TODDLER HOLDING A LOLLIPOP.

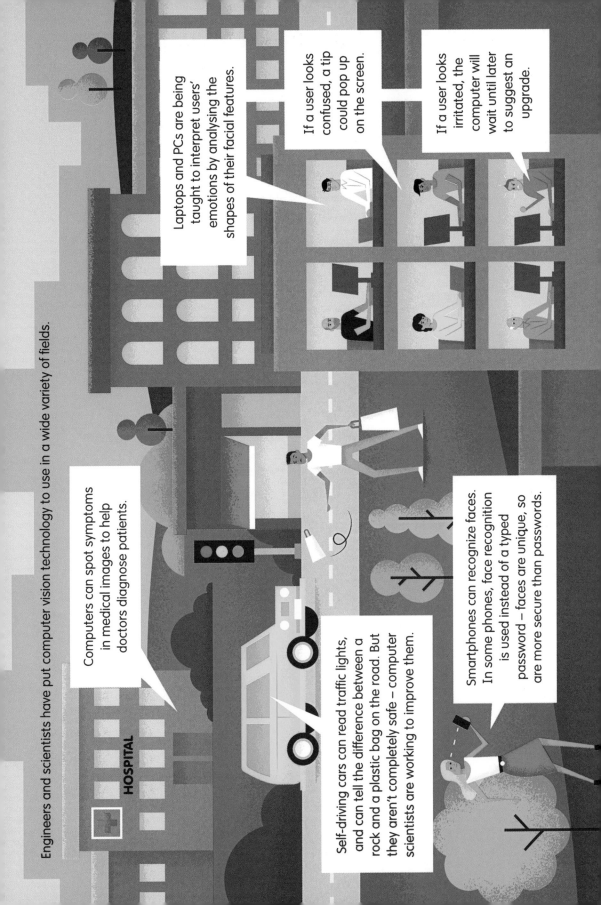

Shuffling cards for years...

will probably never recreate any sequence twice.

Every time someone shuffles a deck of playing cards, the cards fall into a sequence. This specific sequence will almost certainly never happen again, because the number of possible sequences in a deck is so enormous.

This is a deck of 52 cards, the most common kind of deck.

How many possible sequences are there in a 52-card deck?

The number of possible sequences for the whole deck is calculated by multiplying **52 x 51 x 50 x 49** and so on... down to 1.

Why do you multiply the numbers in that way?

There are 52 possible cards that can come first in the sequence...

...there are 51 possible cards that can come second...

...50 possible cards that can come third, 49 that can come fourth, and so on.

The answer is **huge** – it is **68 digits** long:

80,658,175,170,943,878,571,660,
636,856,403,766,975,289,505,440,
883,277,824,000,000,000,000
possible sequences

Let's call this number A.

Wouldn't we create the same sequence again eventually?

Imagine that every single person in the world shuffled a pack of cards every minute of every day.

Together we would complete this many shuffles a year:

7.5 billion people in the world
x   **60 minutes** in an hour
x   **24 hours** in a day
x   **365.25 days** in a year

= **3,944,700,000,000,000**
shuffles per year

Let's call this number B.

So how many years could it take to recreate the sequence?

The number of years it would take is the number of possible sequences (A) divided by the number of shuffles per year (B), which equals:

20,447,226,701,889,600,000,000,000,000,000,000,000,000,000,000,000,000 years

That's far longer than the Universe has even existed. So it's extremely unlikely that shuffling will ever produce the exact sequence on this page.

Unless you're playing cards with a cheat...

46 QWERTY...

is a throwback to the 1870s.

In English-speaking countries, most computer keyboards have a layout called **QWERTY**. One reason for this layout is that when it was devised, it prevented mechanical typewriters from jamming.

1860s
The first typewriters had keys arranged in alphabetical order. When a key on a typewriter was pressed, it moved a metal bar, which stamped a letter in ink on a piece of paper. But the metal bars behind the keys often jammed.

1873
The QWERTY keyboard was designed to space out common combinations of letters, such as S+T and O+N. This stopped the typewriter from jamming.

Over the next 20 years, typewriters improved. Keys were much less likely to jam, so it was no longer necessary to space out common combinations of letters.

This keyboard definitely can't jam. LOL.

But QWERTY typewriters were selling in their thousands, so manufacturers didn't want to change them.

1970s to today
The QWERTY layout was carried through to keyboards in modern electronics, including today's computers and smartphones.

47 Piphilology...

is the art of reciting pi.

The constant **pi** (π) has an infinite number of digits – it goes on forever. This has led to an international quest to learn by heart more digits than anyone else, a skill known as **piphilology**.

3.14159265358979323846264338327950288419716939937510582097494459230781640628620899862803482534211706798214808651328230664709384460955058223172535940812848111745028410270193852110555964462294895493038196442881097566593344612847564822...

In 2015, the Pi World Rankings put Suresh Kumar Sharma as the best, having recited 70,030 digits. It took him 17 hours to recite them all.

People often use a memorization trick called a **piem** – a pi poem – to help them remember the first few digits.

The number of letters of each word of the poem represents each digit.

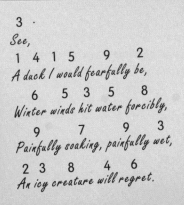

3 .
See,
1 4 1 5   9   2
A duck I would fearfully be,
6   5 3 5   8
Winter winds hit water forcibly,
9   7   9 3
Painfully soaking, painfully wet,
2 3 8   4 6
An icy creature will regret.

48 A tiny spot in your brain...

is dedicated to recognizing numbers.

Scientists have discovered a small area of the brain 0.5cm (0.2in) wide that is used specifically to recognize numbers. It's in a region called the **inferior temporal gyrus,** which is on both sides of the brain just behind your ears.

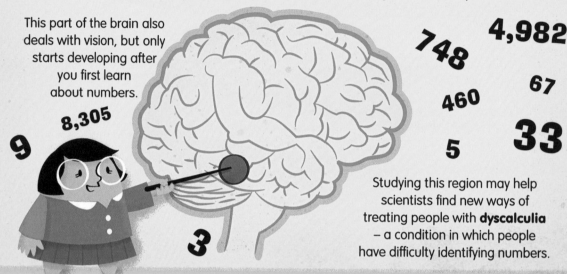

This part of the brain also deals with vision, but only starts developing after you first learn about numbers.

8,305

9

748

4,982

460

67

5

33

3

Studying this region may help scientists find new ways of treating people with **dyscalculia** – a condition in which people have difficulty identifying numbers.

49 There's a little duck...

in every email address.

In many languages, excluding English, the @ ('at') symbol, used in all email addresses, is **zoomorphized** – described as an animal.

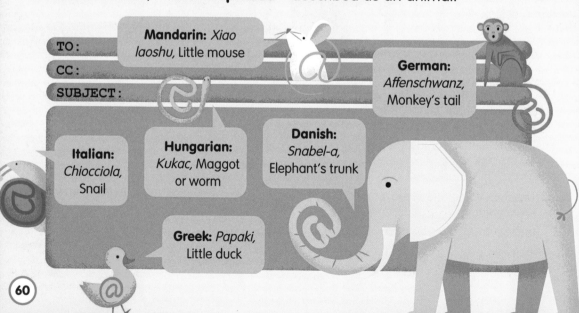

TO :

CC :

SUBJECT :

Mandarin: *Xiao laoshu,* Little mouse

German: *Affenschwanz,* Monkey's tail

Italian: *Chiocciola,* Snail

Hungarian: *Kukac,* Maggot or worm

Danish: *Snabel-a,* Elephant's trunk

Greek: *Papaki,* Little duck

A googolplex has more zeros...

than the Universe has atoms.

A **googolplex** is an unimaginably huge number, created by multiplying 10 by itself lots of times. Follow these simple calculations to see how it adds up.

$$10^1 = 10$$

The small numbers are called **powers**.

10^1 means you multiply by 10 once.

$$10^2 = 10 \times 10$$
$$= 100$$

10^2 means you multiply by 10 twice.

$$10^{10} = 10 \times 10 \times 10 \times 10 \times 10 \times 10 \times 10 \times 10 \times 10 \times 10$$
$$= 10{,}000{,}000{,}000$$

$10^{100} = 10 \times 10 \times 10 \times 10 \times 10 \times 10 \times 10 \times 10 \times 10 \times 10 \times 10 \times 10 \times 10 \times 10 \times$
$10 \times 10 \times 10 \times 10 \times 10 \times 10 \times 10 \times 10 \times 10 \times 10 \times 10 \times 10 \times 10 \times 10 \times 10 \times$
$10 \times 10 \times 10 \times 10 \times 10 \times 10 \times 10 \times 10 \times 10 \times 10 \times 10 \times 10 \times 10 \times 10 \times 10 \times$
$10 \times 10 \times 10 \times 10 \times 10 \times 10 \times 10 \times 10 \times 10 \times 10 \times 10 \times 10 \times 10 \times 10 \times 10 \times$
$10 \times 10 \times 10 \times 10 \times 10 \times 10 \times 10 \times 10 \times 10 \times 10 \times 10 \times 10 \times 10 \times 10 \times 10 \times$
$10 \times 10 \times 10 \times 10 \times 10 \times 10 \times 10 \times 10 \times 10 \times 10 \times 10 \times 10 \times 10 \times 10 \times 10 \times$
$10 \times 10 \times 10 \times 10 \times 10 \times 10 \times 10 \times 10 \times 10 \times 10 \times 10$

This answer is a number called a **googol** – it has 100 zeros...

$$= 10{,}000$$

A **googolplex** is 10^{googol}. It's so big, that it's impossible to write down. A googolplex has more zeros than there are atoms in the entire Universe.

51 Medieval finger reckoners...

could count to a million on their hands.

Ever since people began counting, they have used their fingers to keep track. One of the oldest known methods was recorded by an English monk in the 8th century. He claimed it was possible to count all the way from one to a million, in a system known as **finger reckoning**.

Using only the fingers on the left hand, a person can create at least 99 different patterns. Here's one surviving version:

1	2	3	4	5	10	20

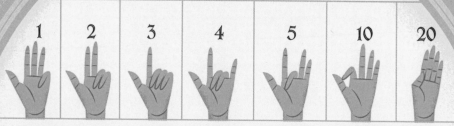

By using the right hand as well, reckoners could count on into the hundreds:

100	101	999

This system allowed people to count every number all the way to 10,000. For large round numbers, reckoners held up their hands in different positions:

1,000,000 was shown by interlocking both hands above the head...

20,000	20,001	40,000

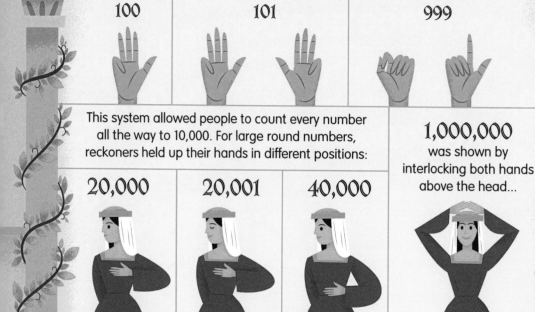

...but people would have needed a second pair of hands to count higher.

A thumb-sized notch...

used to mean a loan of a hundred Pounds.

Between the 12th and 19th centuries, many people in Europe couldn't read or write. Money lenders used wooden receipts, called **split tally sticks**, so that anyone could read them. They were carved with notches to represent the amount of money loaned. Here's how they worked.

1 The borrower and lender agreed the size of the loan.

2 Notches were carved in a piece of wood to represent the amount.

3 Different sizes of notch stood for different amounts.

width of a little finger
20

width of a thumb
100

width of a palm
1,000

4 The carved tally stick was split in two.

1.300

The lender took one half.

The borrower took the other half, and the money.

5 At payback time, the lender and borrower lined up their halves of the split tally stick.

6 The lender checked that the grains of the wood matched, to make sure the borrower hadn't switched their half for one showing a smaller loan.

53 Humans can't beat computers...

in a game of chess.

Even before the first computers were built, engineers wondered if a machine could ever be designed to play a game that required brain power, such as chess. Almost as soon as electronic computers were invented, computer scientists rose to the challenge...

1940s
Computer science pioneer Alan Turing devised a way to program a computer to play chess, but machines at the time didn't have enough memory to run the program.

1957
An *IBM 704* computer became the first to follow a program, play a full game of chess and beat beginner players.

1970s
Chess programs were clever enough to defeat roughly 75% of chess players – all but experts and masters.

1997
Deep Blue, a computer specifically designed to play chess, became the first to defeat a world champion in an official tournament.

2005–present
From this point, the best computers have always been able to defeat the best humans...

...unless they are playing **freestyle chess**. In this version, human players work in teams, and use computers to help.

Even the best chess computer can't defeat a human *and* computer team – yet.

is dreaded in cricket.

An individual or team score of 111 runs in cricket is considered unlucky by some superstitious players. They believe that they are more likely to be out, or that bad things will happen on that score.

A score of 111 is called a *Nelson*, after British hero Lord Nelson, who was said to have lost

1 arm
1 eye
1 leg in battle

(In fact, he never lost a leg.)

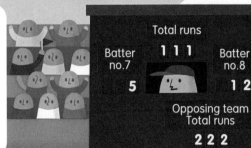

Total runs

1 1 1

Batter no.7

5

Batter no.8

1 2

Opposing team Total runs

2 2 2

A number of teams or individuals have been out with a score of 111. When commentators noticed this, players began to get superstitious.

Scores that are multiples of 111 are also considered bad luck. 222 is known as a *Double Nelson*, 333 as a *Treble Nelson*.

One umpire, named David Shepherd, was known to raise his leg at a score of 111, which drew loud cheers from supporters.

111

Bail

Stump

A batter is called out if the bowler hits the wicket, which is made up of three stumps and two bails.

Some people think that a score of 111 is unlucky because it resembles a wicket without the bails.

they could drive to Neptune in under two minutes.

Since the early 1960s, the *amount* of information that computers are capable of processing, and the *rate* at which they process it, has *doubled* approximately every two years. This phenomenon is known as **Moore's Law**.

To put Moore's Law into perspective:

If the height to which humans can build skyscrapers had increased at the same rate, the tallest skyscraper would now reach further than the Sun.

If a car's top speed had increased at the same rate, the fastest cars would travel faster than the speed of light (which is impossible).

They would be able to reach Neptune in under two minutes.

Early 1960s:	By now:	Early 1960s:	By now:
Tallest skyscraper: Empire State Building	The tallest skyscraper would be over	Fastest car: *Aston DB4 GT Zagato*	The top speed would be approximately
Height: **381m** (1,250ft) tall	**205 billion meters** (672 billion feet) tall.	Top speed: **247km/h (153.5mph)**	**132 billion km/h** (82 billion mph).

But progress in computer processing power has begun to slow down:

SLOW

For Moore's Law to hold true, switches inside computer chips, known as **transistors**, have had to shrink so that more can fit.

They've shrunk so much that the smallest are now only a few atoms thick.

It's becoming *physically impossible* to make them much smaller.

So what next?

Many computer scientists believe that new ways of computing must be invented for progress to keep going at the rate it has been.

But nobody yet knows what they might be.

One thing we do know:

If Moore's Law were to continue, in 200 years a laptop-sized computer would be able to process information at such a high rate...

...it would need a power supply equivalent to the energy released by a **medium-sized star**.

Physicists have calculated that a processing rate that high is the absolute upper limit physically possible for a computer of that size.

56 19th-century codes...

may hide a hoard of buried treasure.

In 1885, a pamphlet was published in the US containing three codes. The author claimed that cracking all the codes would reveal the location and contents of a huge stash of buried treasure.

CRACK THREE CODES   **FIND THE TREASURE!**

One of the codes was cracked using the American Declaration of Independence.

115 73 24 807 37 52 49 17 31 62 647
22 7 15 140 47 29 107 79 84 56 239
10 26 811 5 196 308 85 52

Each number in the code related to a word in the Declaration, for example the number 5 meant the fifth word of the declaration.

AMERICAN DECLARATION OF INDEPENDENCE

WHEN IN THE COURSE OF HUMAN EVENTS IT BECOMES NECESSARY FOR ONE PEOPLE TO DISSOLVE THE POLITICAL BANDS...

Taking the first letter from each of these words and stringing them together, spelled out a message.

The message revealed that the treasure was gold, silver and jewels.

Generations of cryptographers have attempted to solve the other two codes, but they remain unbroken.

Many people think the whole thing might simply be an elaborate hoax.

57 Jumping an air gap...

is a hacker's greatest challenge.

Hackers are people who try to access files on other people's computers without them knowing. Virtually all modern computers are connected to the internet automatically, giving hackers a way in. Some computers are shielded from internet access by something called an **air gap**.

Places such as nuclear power stations and military headquarters use air gap computers, and keep them in ultra-secure locations. These computers never connect to the internet.

Only authorized people can touch those computers. Any information they hold cannot be accessed or tampered with wirelessly.

The term 'air gap' comes from a time before wireless internet connections such as Wifi existed. Then computers needed a physical cable to connect to a wall socket.

In movies, hackers might try to sneak into the room where an air gap computer is hidden.

 But in real life, successful hackers simply trick an authorized person, for example by giving them a USB stick with hidden programs or viruses. By plugging the USB into a machine, it allows hackers to steal information.

58 Badly written code...

can be like spaghetti.

A well-written computer program should be easy for other coders to follow. If a program is so badly written, or **tangled**, that other coders find it hard to read, it's described as **spaghetti code**.

Here's how a program becomes **spaghettified**:

| A computer program is made up of lots of instructions. | The order in which the instructions are carried out is known as the **control flow**. | Instructions in well-written code are organized to make the control flow easy to follow. |

But certain types of instruction make the control flow more complicated.

An instruction that forces the computer to make a decision is known as an **If-then-else statement**.

An instruction that makes the control flow jump to another part of the program, often skipping some steps, is known as a **GOTO statement**.

GOTOs and If-then-else statements aren't always bad – sometimes they're needed. But too many jumps and decisions together make a program almost impossible to follow.

If it's unclear how all of the instructions are connected, it's hard to make changes without accidentally messing up another part of the program.

59 Copying and pasting files...

has led to a new religion.

Kopimism was officially declared a religion in Sweden in 2012.
Kopimists believe all information should be shared,
and that copying digital files is a sacred act.

There has even been a Kopimist wedding in Serbia in 2012, in which a projector
beamed Kopimist symbols onto a wall while a computer read out the vows.

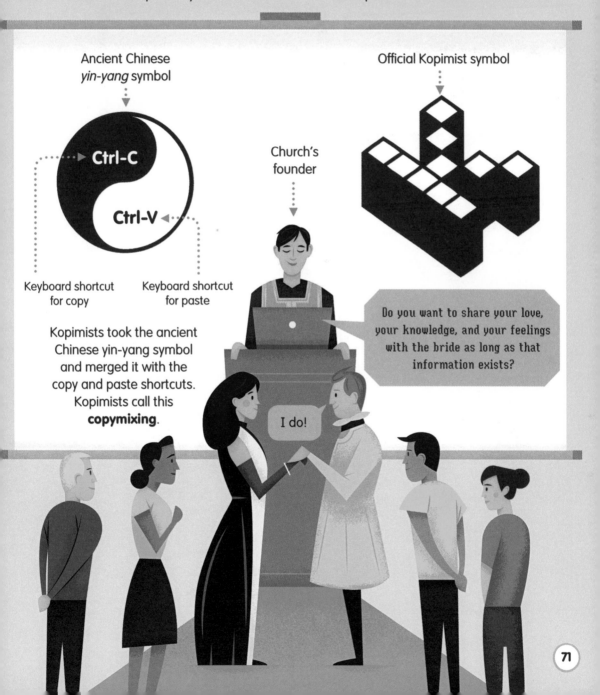

Ancient Chinese
yin-yang symbol

Official Kopimist symbol

Ctrl-C

Ctrl-V

Church's
founder

Keyboard shortcut
for copy

Keyboard shortcut
for paste

Kopimists took the ancient
Chinese yin-yang symbol
and merged it with the
copy and paste shortcuts.
Kopimists call this
copymixing.

Do you want to share your love,
your knowledge, and your feelings
with the bride as long as that
information exists?

I do!

60 Books could grow on trees...

by planting digital data in seeds.

Millions of books and documents are stored as **computer data** in online archives and libraries. Scientists known as **biotechnologists** have found a way to translate this data into chemical data in plants, so that the books and documents can be stored in seeds instead.

Data on a computer is stored as **bits**. These can be grouped in pairs, with four possible pairs: 00, 01, 10 and 11.

Plant cells store information as a chemical called **DNA**. It's made up of four different chemical components known as A, C, T and G.

Biotechnologists have noticed that there are four options in each case, and written a code, in which...

00 = A

01 = T

10 = C

11 = G

From this code it is possible to create artificial DNA in which the sequence of chemicals matches the bits in a set of computer data.

61 A billionaire in France...

is richer than a billionaire in Ireland.

France and the Republic of Ireland have the same currency, the Euro, but use different systems for naming very large numbers. France uses **long scale**, while Ireland uses **short scale**. Here's how they compare.

In short scale, every new word greater than 'million' is **one thousand** times larger than the previous term.

I'm a billionaire!

No, *I'm* a billionaire!

In long scale, every new word is **one million** times larger.

SHORT SCALE				LONG SCALE
Million	Million	1,000,000	Million	
Billion	Billion	1,000,000,000		
	Trillion	1,000,000,000,000	Billion	
	Quadrillion	1,000,000,000,000,000		
	Quintillion	1,000,000,000,000,000,000	Trillion	

62 Adding numbers to bank notes...

doesn't always buy you more.

Between 2004 and 2008, an economic crisis in Zimbabwe caused prices to rocket. This is known as **hyperinflation**. So that people didn't have to carry around bucketfuls of cash to buy everyday items, the government printed bank notes with much larger numbers on them.

One of the largest numbers ever printed on a bank note was **100 trillion** Zimbabwean Dollars.

RESERVE BANK OF ZIMBABWE

ONE HUNDRED TRILLION DOLLARS

When the crisis was at its worst, a 100 trillion dollar note couldn't even buy you a bus ticket in Harare, Zimbabwe's capital city.

63 One millinillion squared...

equals one billimillion.

There is a set of grammar rules, known as the **Conway-Wechsler system**, that determines the names for very, VERY, large numbers. But some of the names are very long themselves.

One millinillion is one followed by 3,003 zeros, or $10^{3,003}$.

Multiplying it by itself, or **squaring** it, gives one billimillion.

But those names are incredibly short in comparison to some...

One quattuorquinquagintaquadringentillion today!

Happy 10^{1365}th birthday!

That's over two hundred quinquagintaquadringentillion times older than Earth.

64 Secret codes of battle...

were hidden on leather belts.

Ancient Greek soldiers used wooden sticks called **scytales** to encode battle information. A scytale message could be written on a soldier's belt.

Instructions for using your scytale:

①

Make sure you and the recipient of your message
have scytales of the same thickness.

②

Wrap the belt around the scytale to write out your message.

W	E	W	I	L	L
A	T	T	A	C	K
A	T	D	A	W	N

③

Then unwind it. This is what the encrypted message would look like.

④

Deliver your belt to the appropriate person –
usually a commander or chief.

He winds the belt around his scytale
to reveal the message.

⑤

ATTACK!

This type of encryption, where letters are shifted according to set rules, is called **transposition**.
In the centuries that followed, wartime encryption became increasingly complicated...

65 Secret codes of war...

were set using plugs and wheels.

During the Second World War (1939-1945), the German military encoded radio messages using a mechanical encryption machine called **Enigma**. It used a complicated system of **substitutions** – turning one letter into another.

WE WILL ATTACK AT DAWN

First, the machine was set up by turning **rotor wheels** and changing a **plugboard** according to decided settings.

Rotor wheels

Lampboard

Keyboard

Plugboard

Then the message was typed out on a **keyboard**.

Each pressed key lit up a letter on the **lampboard**, making up the final coded message.

IJAHKFOBAUXUOHPLXZ

The person receiving the message was instructed to set their plugboard and rotor wheels to the same settings as the sender. Inputting the encrypted sequence would then reveal the original message.

Enigma was almost impossible to crack because it could have over **150 quintillion** (150 million million million) different settings.

Cracking the code required the invention of a new machine – the huge **Bombe** – by **Alan Turing**, one of the first computer scientists.

66 A mathematical mystery...

saved a man's life.

One day, in the late 1800s...

The story goes that a German businessman named **Paul Wolfskehl** declared his love for a woman.

But she said she didn't love him back.

Brokenhearted, he planned to kill himself at the stroke of midnight. To pass the time until then, he read about a math problem which had fascinated him for years.

The problem was known as **Fermat's Last Theorem**.

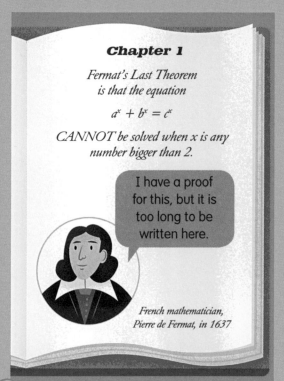

Chapter 1

Fermat's Last Theorem is that the equation

$$a^x + b^x = c^x$$

CANNOT be solved when x is any number bigger than 2.

> I have a proof for this, but it is too long to be written here.

French mathematician, Pierre de Fermat, in 1637

The next morning...

FERMAT'S THEOREM

> What is love compared to mathematical beauty?

Wolfskehl became so absorbed in trying to figure out Fermat's proof that he missed midnight. The problem had given him a new lease on life.

Wolfskehl was just one of many math lovers who worked on the problem. However, it remained unsolved. When he died many years later, his will stated:

> To whomever proves Fermat's theorem, I bequeath the sum of 100,000 Marks.

Cambridge, UK, 1993...

Over 100 years later, British mathematician **Andrew Wiles** stood up in front of prominent mathematicians from around the world, and wrote out a proof of Fermat's Theorem.

Newspapers hailed it as a huge victory, and Wiles became a celebrity almost overnight.

Greatest mathematician of the century

MATH MYSTERY SOLVED!

Before Wiles could claim the prize, every calculation in his 129-page proof was checked. But a mistake was found.

ERROR

Facing a humiliating backlash, Wiles shut himself away. For the next 14 months, he worked tirelessly, trying to salvage his proof.

In 1994, Wiles finally cracked it and won the reward. But he'd had to use mathematical techniques only developed in the 20th century, including some he had invented himself.

Fermat couldn't have known these techniques, and mathematicians now wonder whether he actually did find a proof of his own...

67 A triangle of numbers...

has the answers to certain mathematical questions.

This number triangle is known as **Pascal's Triangle**.

Below you can find out how to use it.

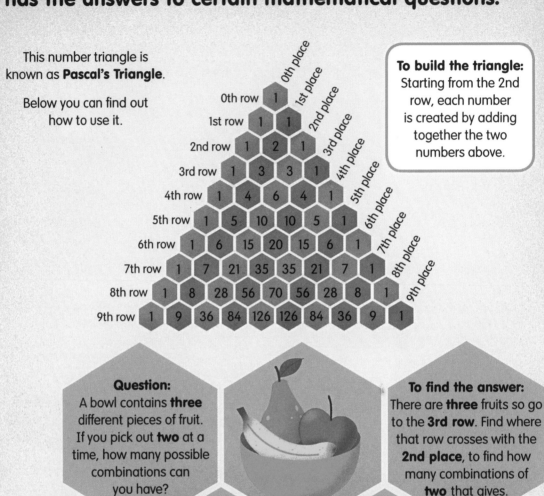

To build the triangle: Starting from the 2nd row, each number is created by adding together the two numbers above.

0th row — 1
1st row — 1 1
2nd row — 1 2 1
3rd row — 1 3 3 1
4th row — 1 4 6 4 1
5th row — 1 5 10 10 5 1
6th row — 1 6 15 20 15 6 1
7th row — 1 7 21 35 35 21 7 1
8th row — 1 8 28 56 70 56 28 8 1
9th row — 1 9 36 84 126 126 84 36 9 1

0th place, 1st place, 2nd place, 3rd place, 4th place, 5th place, 6th place, 7th place, 8th place, 9th place

Question:
A bowl contains **three** different pieces of fruit. If you pick out **two** at a time, how many possible combinations can you have?

To find the answer:
There are **three** fruits so go to the **3rd row**. Find where that row crosses with the **2nd place**, to find how many combinations of **two** that gives.

3rd row

1
1 1
1 2 1
1 3 3 1
1 4 6 4 1

2nd place

Answer:
3

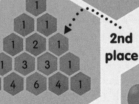

Now see if you can answer these questions using Pascal's Triangle...

1
If you have seven fruits, how many combinations of five fruits can you have?

2
How many combinations of three fruits can you make from a bowl of nine?

Answers:
1. 7th row, 5th place = 21
2. 9th row, 3rd place = 84

68 Ding, dong, dang, bing, bong...

can be rung 120 different ways.

In 17th-century England, church bell ringers developed a new style of ringing multiple bells in sequence. This was not based on music but on a mathematical pattern.

Dong Ding
Ding Dong

A church with 2 bells can ring its bells in just **2** sequences.
(2 x 1)

Ding Dong Dang
Dang Ding Dong
Ding Dang Dong

Dang Dong Ding
Dong Dang Ding
Dong Ding Dang

A church with 3 bells can ring its bells in **6** sequences.
(3 x 2 x 1)

Dong Dang Ding Bing Bong
Dong Ding Dang Bong Bing

Ding Dong Dang Bong Bing
Bing Dong Ding Dang Bong

A church with 5 bells can ring its bells in **120** different sequences.
(5 x 4 x 3 x 2 x 1)

Expert bell ringers wrote manuals explaining how to play out a full set of sequences without repeating any. The first two of these books were called *Tintinnalogia* and *Campanalogia*. Today, the style is known as **change-ringing**.

Ringing a complete set of sequences is traditionally known as **pealing** the bells. A single peal can take hours if a church has 7 bells, which requires **5,040** unique sequences.
(7 x 6 x 5 x 4 x 3 x 2 x 1)

69 The world's deadliest code...

is hidden on a biscuit.

The President of the United States of America has access to a secret code, on a card called '**the biscuit**'. In the event of a nuclear attack, it would be used to release powerful nuclear weapons.

The President has possession of the biscuit at all times. The code is a way to identify the President, so no one else can order an attack. The numbers and letters, known as **Gold Codes**, are changed every day.

Gold Codes activate *other* codes kept inside a briefcase called the **nuclear football**, carried by military aides.

SHTIR49832DJE
9RIKTSN37DFJA

The biscuit looks rather like a credit card.

It contains meaningless numbers and letters too, so even if a thief got hold of it, they wouldn't be able to find the actual code.

Only the US Security Services actually know what the Gold Codes look like. We're just guessing.

can become zombies.

Sometimes criminals hack into and take over people's computers and use them to attack websites. The computer that's been taken over is called a **zombie**. The criminal in charge of a network of zombies is called a **bot herder**.

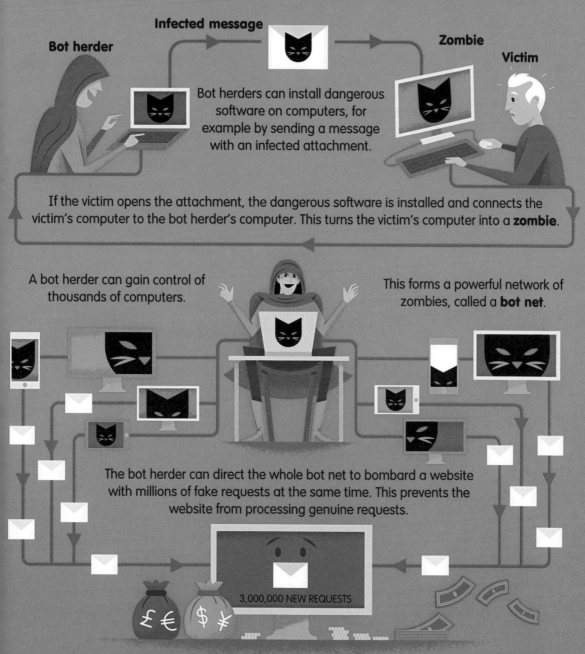

Infected message

Bot herder

Zombie

Victim

Bot herders can install dangerous software on computers, for example by sending a message with an infected attachment.

If the victim opens the attachment, the dangerous software is installed and connects the victim's computer to the bot herder's computer. This turns the victim's computer into a **zombie**.

A bot herder can gain control of thousands of computers.

This forms a powerful network of zombies, called a **bot net**.

The bot herder can direct the whole bot net to bombard a website with millions of fake requests at the same time. This prevents the website from processing genuine requests.

3,000,000 NEW REQUESTS

In 2017, a bot herder crashed the online services of three British banks. The bot herder asked for £75,000 to call off the attack. The banks didn't pay, and the bot herder was arrested.

71 Origami in space...

helps solar panels to open and close.

Origami is the ancient Japanese art of paper folding. In 1985, Japanese astrophysicist **Koriyo Miura** used origami and geometry to devise a new way of folding paper that has been used to make foldable solar panels for satellites in space.

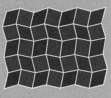

The **Miura fold** pattern is made up of interlocking shapes, known as parallelograms.

This kind of repeated pattern, without gaps or overlaps, is called **tessellation**.

MIURA FOLD INSTRUCTIONS

1 Fold a piece of paper into 5 equal strips, alternating the direction of each fold.

2 Fold the paper along these creases to make a strip.

------ Mountain fold
------ Valley fold

3 Fold this strip at an angle.

4 Fold it again, alternating the direction of the fold.

Make these ...▶ edges parallel as you fold.
:......▶

5 Continue making folds in this way...

...until you have 6 folds.

6 Unfold the paper, then refold on the zig-zag creases, alternating mountain folds with valley folds.

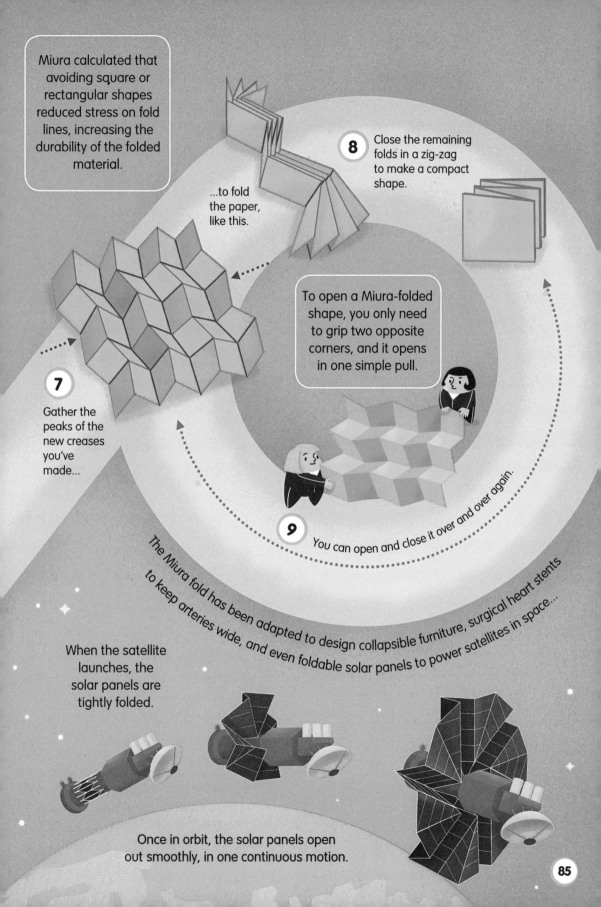

Miura calculated that avoiding square or rectangular shapes reduced stress on fold lines, increasing the durability of the folded material.

...to fold the paper, like this.

8 Close the remaining folds in a zig-zag to make a compact shape.

To open a Miura-folded shape, you only need to grip two opposite corners, and it opens in one simple pull.

7 Gather the peaks of the new creases you've made...

9 You can open and close it over and over again.

The Miura fold has been adapted to design collapsible furniture, surgical heart stents to keep arteries wide, and even foldable solar panels to power satellites in space...

When the satellite launches, the solar panels are tightly folded.

Once in orbit, the solar panels open out smoothly, in one continuous motion.

could make you rich.

In 2009, an unknown person or organization released the first currency that only exists online. It's known as a **cryptocurrency**. Cryptocurrencies are accessed online by a process called **mining**.

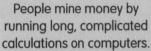
People mine money by running long, complicated calculations on computers.

Each time a user finds a new solution to these calculations, they are said to have 'mined' a unit of money, or 'coin'.

Cryptocurrencies can be used to buy things online, or traded to make more money.

In theory, a cryptocurrency is something that anyone could use, anywhere in the world. It doesn't rely on a central bank or organization, nor does it depend on the wealth of a particular country.

Some cryptocurrencies, such as **Bitcoin**, are extremely valuable because it's very difficult to mine new coins. There are a finite number of bitcoins – 21 million – out there, waiting to be found.

When they first appeared in 2009, each Bitcoin was worth about **$0.30 (£0.18)**. At their peak in 2017, each Bitcoin was worth **$19,665 (£14,760)** – more than 15 ounces of gold.

73 Soccer statistics...

turn games into numbers.

Mathematicians are revolutionizing top soccer teams. Data from every match is analyzed in minute detail to monitor players' performances, plan training regimes and devise the best strategy for winning games.

Statisticians look at more than 1,000 factors from each match. They create a numerical picture of each game and look for patterns in the data.

Data for each player
Average pass length
Key contributions
Shots on target
Sprints per game
Completed passes
Distance per game

Data shows goalkeepers are twice as likely to dive to their right to save a goal if their team is losing.

90°

25°

Mathematicians have calculated that shots using wider angles of coverage are more effective for scoring goals.

Players who can sprint faster for longer are more likely to score goals.

Top sprint speed:
32km/h (19.9mph)

45°

Optimum kicking angle for long kicks: 45°

Managers use the data to analyze which passes work best, and where each player is best positioned in each game.

But not everything can be measured in numbers. Observation may still be best for assessing psychological factors, such as a player's positive attitude.

74 The most distant computer...

takes over 19 hours to send information to Earth.

Voyager 1, an American spacecraft launched in 1977, is exploring the outer reaches of our Solar System. It has computers on board that send regular data to Earth. But it's so far away that its messages take almost a day to reach Earth.

Computers at NASA, America's space agency, pick up signals from *Voyager 1* using giant antennae.

Earth

75 Flashes and clicks...

can be letters and numbers.

An international language called **Morse code** has been used to send messages for the last 160 years. Letters and numbers are turned into combinations of **dots and dashes**, usually sent as flashes, clicks or beeps.

This is a dot. It's a short flash or sound.

This is a dash. It's three times the length of a dot.

Sensors record data about magnetic fields, radiation and particles from stars in space.

Three computers on board convert data into radio signals.

Voyager 1 transmits radio signals to Earth every day. These currently take 19 hours to reach Earth.

Voyager 1 is more than 21 billion km (13 billion miles) from Earth, further than any other man-made object. As it moves further away, its messages will take longer and longer to reach Earth.

Workers at NASA send commands to *Voyager 1* telling it when to send its data.

Morse code can be used to send secret messages in wartime, signal to ships out at sea, or send silent signals on camping trips...

HELLO

What you click on today...

will influence what you see tomorrow.

Some websites use programs to analyze everything you do online. By tracking what you search for and click on, these programs assess what you like and dislike, and decide what you might want to see next. The search results selected for you are known as your **filter bubble**.

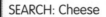

SEARCH: Cheese

Different users can use the same search word, but get different results, based on their previous searches.

Great cheese deals at your local store.

I ♥ CHEESE

Watch cheese rolling LIVE!

A day in the life of a cheese sculptor.

The scary truth about dairy farms.

Ten cheeses that taste like feet.

I dumped my partner because he loves cheese.

Many people think filter bubbles are a problem. If you only see things that the programs *think* you like, you're less likely to come across new ideas.

Bubblegum flavored cheese invented in Finland.

In turn, if you get used to liking what you see, you might stop questioning what you read, and believe false information, sometimes called **fake news**.

Cheddar tree discovered in Amazon Rainforest.

Gouda is radioactive, scientists confirm.

Bursting your filter bubble allows you to come across a wider range of ideas. You can do this by searching things you've never searched for before.

77 By the time you've read this line...

over 30 million emails will have been sent.

With about 3.7 billion users worldwide, the internet is processing a colossal amount of data every day. Here's some of what happens in just 10 seconds.

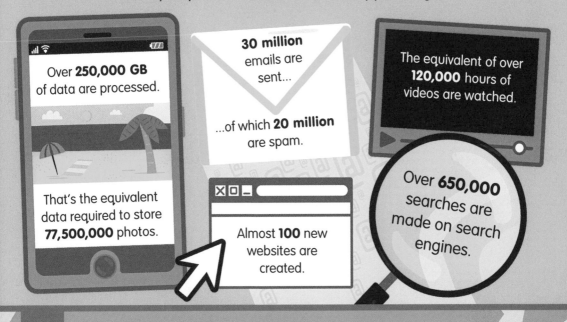

Over **250,000 GB** of data are processed.

That's the equivalent data required to store **77,500,000** photos.

30 million emails are sent...

...of which **20 million** are spam.

Almost **100** new websites are created.

The equivalent of over **120,000** hours of videos are watched.

Over **650,000** searches are made on search engines.

78 It only takes four colors...

to shade a map.

In 1852, mathematician **Francis Guthrie** noticed that it took just four colors to fill in a map of the British counties *without a color touching itself*. He set out to prove that four colors were all you needed for *any* map.

In 1976, mathematicians finally proved Guthrie was right. It is now called the **Four Color Theorem**.

This applies to all maps or random pictures that are split into many sections.

It was the first major theorem to be proved using a computer. It took the computer 1,000 hours to run all the calculations necessary for the proof.

79 Numbers can save lives...

by predicting the future.

Collecting numbers about current weather patterns can help us predict the weather. This allows countries to make plans for natural disasters, such as hurricanes or floods, which can save peoples' lives.

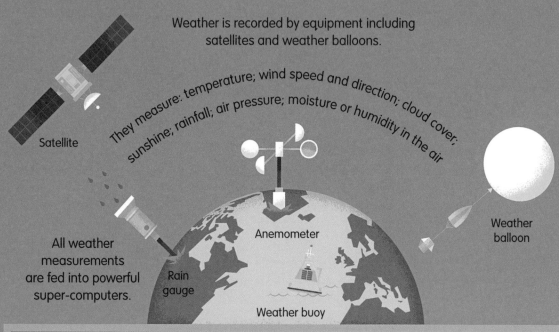

Weather is recorded by equipment including satellites and weather balloons.

They measure: temperature; wind speed and direction; cloud cover; sunshine; rainfall; air pressure; moisture or humidity in the air

Satellite

Anemometer

Weather balloon

All weather measurements are fed into powerful super-computers.

Rain gauge

Weather buoy

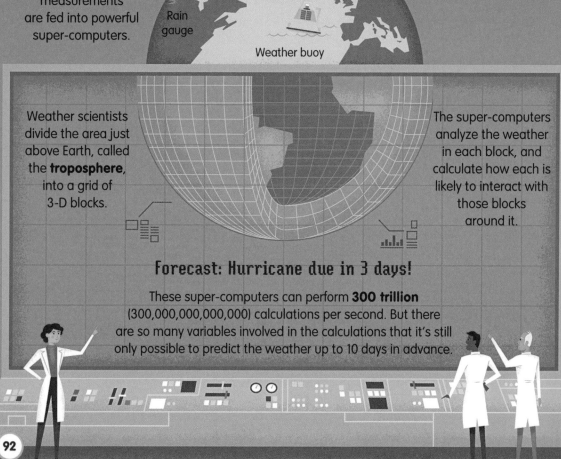

Weather scientists divide the area just above Earth, called the **troposphere**, into a grid of 3-D blocks.

The super-computers analyze the weather in each block, and calculate how each is likely to interact with those blocks around it.

Forecast: Hurricane due in 3 days!

These super-computers can perform **300 trillion** (300,000,000,000,000) calculations per second. But there are so many variables involved in the calculations that it's still only possible to predict the weather up to 10 days in advance.

80 Amicable numbers...

could bring you love.

Ancient Greek mathematicians discovered an extraordinary pair of numbers, that they called **amicable numbers**. The numbers were 220 and 284 – and they became symbols of love.

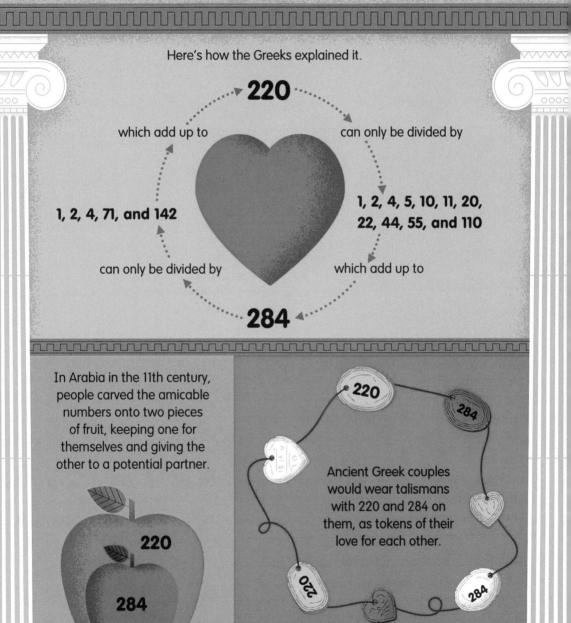

Here's how the Greeks explained it.

220

which add up to → can only be divided by

1, 2, 4, 71, and 142 → 1, 2, 4, 5, 10, 11, 20, 22, 44, 55, and 110

can only be divided by → which add up to

284

In Arabia in the 11th century, people carved the amicable numbers onto two pieces of fruit, keeping one for themselves and giving the other to a potential partner.

220
284

220
284

Ancient Greek couples would wear talismans with 220 and 284 on them, as tokens of their love for each other.

220
284

Though they're not the only pair, 220 and 284 are the smallest amicable numbers. A second pair – 17,296 and 18,416 – wasn't discovered for over a thousand years.

81 Storing data as qubits...

could create the world's most powerful computer.

Computer scientists believe it is possible to build a new kind of computer far more powerful than any that already exists. The key to its power lies in how it stores and processes information. Ordinary computers store information as **bits**, but these new computers will use **qubits** instead.

In most computers, data is stored in millions of switches called transistors, which can be *either* 'on' or 'off' at any one time.

'On' and 'off' represent one of two possibilities: '1' or '0'. A single 1 or 0 is called a **bit**.

Qubits can represent 0 or 1 too. Unlike bits, they can also represent **both at the same time**.

Wait, what? But how?

1

Qubits rely on things far smaller than transistors: the particles that make up atoms.

3

This spin is an example of a **quantum property**. It can be used to build **quantum computers** that can deal with far more information than a laptop or smartphone.

2

These tiny particles behave unlike anything in the visible world. For example, they spin in two directions at once. This gives single qubits the power to process multiple pieces of information simultaneously.

82 Sub-zero temperatures...

could hold the key to quantum supremacy.

Scientists around the world are still striving to build a quantum computer more powerful than an ordinary computer. If and when they achieve this, they will have reached what they call **quantum supremacy**.

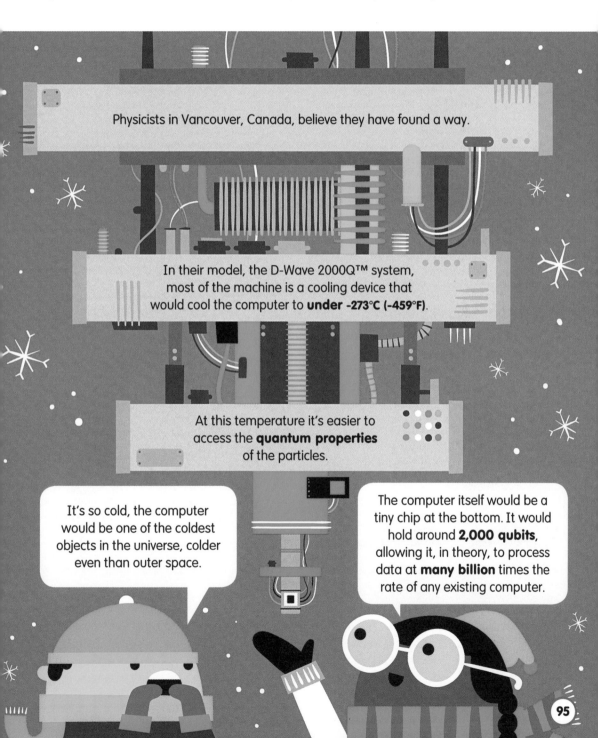

Physicists in Vancouver, Canada, believe they have found a way.

In their model, the D-Wave 2000Q™ system, most of the machine is a cooling device that would cool the computer to **under -273°C (-459°F)**.

At this temperature it's easier to access the **quantum properties** of the particles.

It's so cold, the computer would be one of the coldest objects in the universe, colder even than outer space.

The computer itself would be a tiny chip at the bottom. It would hold around **2,000 qubits**, allowing it, in theory, to process data at **many billion** times the rate of any existing computer.

83 Calculus was invented...

by Isaac Newton.

One of the greatest inventions of the 17th century was a branch of mathematics known as **calculus**. People in Britain claimed the idea was originally **Isaac Newton's**, a British scientist, who described it as 'the method of fluxions'.

1642
Newton was born in Lincolnshire, England.

1665
Newton wrote his earliest notes about 'fluxions'.

1666 – 1675
Newton exchanged letters, and ideas, with German mathematician Gottfried Leibniz.

Newton completed a book describing fluxions, but did not publish it. **1671**

What's calculus for?

Mathematicians use calculus to describe how things change over time – for example the path taken by a cannonball as it flies, or the changes in the price of food in a supermarket over a year.

Often, mathematicians use calculus to draw graphs, with a line showing the pattern of a change. Calculus also provides a way to figure out the exact size of a space underneath a curved line.

1687
Newton published his greatest work, a book called *Principia Mathematica*. It mentioned fluxions briefly.

1693
Newton finally published his notes on fluxions, in part to demonstrate that he had come up with the idea first.

84 Calculus was invented...

by Gottfried Leibniz.

One of the greatest inventions of the 17th century was a branch of mathematics known as **calculus**. It was named by German mathematician **Gottfried Leibniz**, whose methods are still used today. But, by the end of his life, rivals claimed he had stolen his ideas from Isaac Newton.

1666 – 1675
Leibniz exchanged letters and ideas with British mathematician Isaac Newton.

1672
Leibniz moved to Paris to study with leading mathematicians of the day.

1646
Leibniz was born in Leipzig, Saxony.

$$\frac{dy}{dx} \qquad \frac{d^2y}{dx^2}$$

1675
Leibniz wrote his basic notes about calculus, including a way to write it down using letters and numbers.

1677
Leibniz shared his ideas with Newton in a private letter.

1684
Leibniz published his description of calculus.

1690s
Leibniz maintained that he had developed his own ideas independently of Newton. The name 'calculus' and Leibniz's way of writing it down became the mathematical standard.

1715
The British Royal Society officially credited Newton with the invention of calculus.

Today
Historians now agree that Newton had the idea first, but many maintain that Leibniz came up with his own version of calculus by himself.

A fly on the ceiling...

helped people find their way in the world.

When 17th-century French mathematician **René Descartes** was lying in bed one morning, legend has it that he spotted a fly on the ceiling, and thought about how best to describe its location.

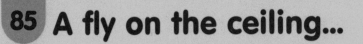

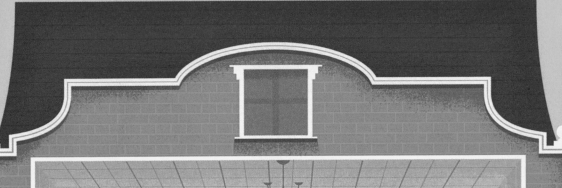

Fixed point

1 According to the story, Descartes described the fly's location by counting the number of steps up and along from a fixed point.

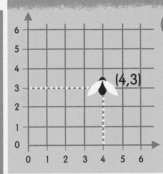

2 Descartes realized he could describe the position of any point on a flat plane using two numbers. These came to be known as **cartesian coordinates** after Descartes' name.

3 This grid system, or graph, is a mathematical way of showing the fly's position.

The coordinates (4,3) describe a point four steps to the right and three steps up from a fixed point, (0,0).

(4,3)

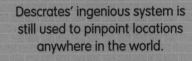

Descrates' ingenious system is still used to pinpoint locations anywhere in the world.

86 A magic square...

stopped a mythical deluge.

1 According to an ancient legend, floods were once devastating China. The Emperor left many gifts for the River God, to try to make the floods stop.

2 As the floods raged, the Emperor saw a giant turtle crawling from the river.

3 Each segment of its shell contained a different number of dots, from one to nine.

4

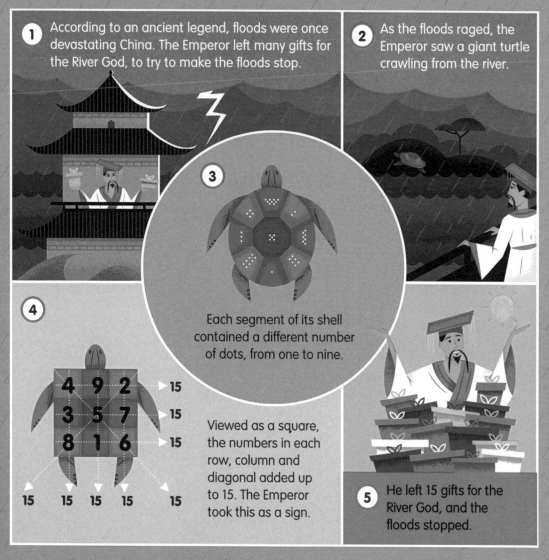

4	9	2	→ 15
3	5	7	→ 15
8	1	6	→ 15

15   15   15   15   15

Viewed as a square, the numbers in each row, column and diagonal added up to 15. The Emperor took this as a sign.

5 He left 15 gifts for the River God, and the floods stopped.

Number patterns like this are called **magic squares**.
They appear in designs and lucky charms from cultures around the world.

A dish with Arabic writing, made in the 18th century

A 17th-century Hebrew charm

Carved into the wall of a 20th-century cathedral in Spain

1	14	14	4
11	7	6	9
8	10	10	5
13	2	3	15

Calculators are more powerful...

than the computers that took men to the Moon.

The computer on board the *Apollo 11* space rocket was responsible for navigating to the Moon, controlling the first ever landing, and coordinating the return journey to Earth. But it was less powerful than some calculators are today.

The 'powerfulness' of an electronic device is called its **processing power**. It's a measure of how many operations it can perform in a certain amount of time. There are two ways to measure it.

$3 + 17 \times 8 - 4 + 26 \div 2 \times 148...$

RAM

RAM (short for random access memory) is how many numbers a computer can hold at once. It is measured in megabytes (MB).

MHz

MHz, or mega hertz, is a measure of the speed at which a computer carries out calculations.

This shows the processing power of four different devices. The columns of blue squares show the amount of RAM and the dials show the speed.

0.004MB of RAM

0.032MB of RAM

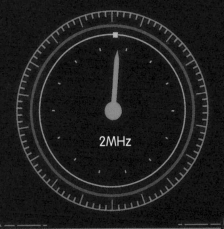

2MHz

Apollo Guidance Computer (1969)

6MHz

Ti-83 scientific calculator (1996)

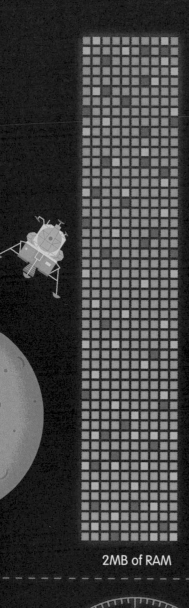

Smartphones today have
such a large amount of RAM
that this column would be
too big to fit on the page.
In fact it would cover every
page in this book.

2MB of RAM

2,000MB of RAM

34MHz

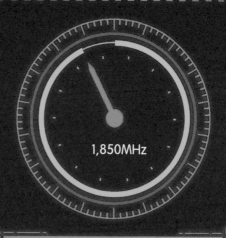

1,850MHz

PS one (2000)

A smartphone (2017)

Bots outnumber humans...

on the internet.

More than half of all website visits aren't by humans, but by **bots**. A bot is software that can run on its own, doing the same task over and over and over again. Different bots do different tasks, and can be either good or bad.

Good bots

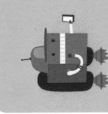

Feed fetcher bots support the app version of a website. They bring information to the app from the main site each time the app is refreshed.

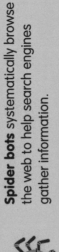

Spider bots systematically browse the web to help search engines gather information.

Good scrapers extract data from websites *with* permission from the website owner, for example to collate flight options on a comparison website.

Health checker bots monitor websites to make sure they are working properly.

Bad bots

Impersonator bots pretend to be humans or good bots. This stops them from being blocked by a website's security settings. If they get through, they can attack a site, putting it out of service.

Hacker bots scour the internet looking for gaps in a website's security. If they find the right gap, they inject code into sites and take them over.

Bad scrapers extract data from websites *without* permission from the website owner. They may steal information from one website and publish it on another.

Website visits in 2016:

48% of website visits were by humans.

29% of web visits were by bad bots.

23% of web visits were by good bots.

69 You can wear computers...

all over your body.

Designers have developed clothing, called **wearables** or **e-textiles**, with built-in computer technology.

Here are some examples on display at a fashion show.

Camera drone ·········▶

My dress is connected wirelessly to my phone. It lights up blue whenever I get a call.

I'm deaf, but this CuteCircuit Soundshirt allows me to *feel* music. It receives music wirelessly and then loosens, tightens and vibrates in response to the sounds.

Ring ring!

This ring can track my sleep patterns.

90 Numbers explain everything...

according to Pythagoras.

Pythagoras was an Ancient Greek mathematician, philosopher and teacher who set up a school over 2,500 years ago. He believed that everything in the Universe, from music to geometry, could be explained by numbers.

Pythagoras gave numbers special characteristics:

In music, he found a link between the lengths of strings on musical instruments and the sounds they produced when plucked.

While in geometry, he found that relationships between numbers could be used to find lengths and shapes, and the distance between stars and planets in the Universe.

1 The number of reason

2 The number of opinion, the symbol of woman

Pythagoras is best known for formulating a theorem about right-angled triangles, although he was not the first to discover it.

3 The number of harmony, the symbol of man

4 The number of justice

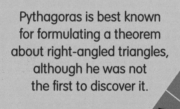

a^2
(a x a)

c^2
(c x c)

c

a

5 The number of marriage, 2 + 3

The sum of the area of the squares on the two smaller sides of the triangle is equal to the area of the square on the longest side. So here, 9 + 16 = 25.

b

b^2
(b x b)

Pythagoras's theorem

$$a^2 + b^2 = c^2$$

for discovering a dangerous type of number.

Legend has it that one of Pythagoras's followers found a number that could not be written like other numbers. His fellow mathematicians were so horrified by this challenge to their way of thinking, they pushed him off a boat to stop him from spreading more ideas.

Pythagoras believed that the Universe was built around **rational** numbers. These are whole numbers or numbers that can be written as fractions.

Rational numbers

18    $\frac{1}{3}$ $3\frac{1}{7}$ 2 $\frac{3}{4}$ 5   76   109

$\frac{7}{10}$

The drowned mathematician, thought to be a man named Hippasus, discovered a number that couldn't be written as a rational number or fraction.

For example, the square root of 2, written **√2**, is a number that when multiplied by itself = 2. This number is:

1.41421356237309

50488016887242096

80785696718753769480731766

79737990732478462107038850387

343276415727350138462309122970249248360560 and on and on and on...

Hippasus deduced that some numbers *weren't* rational, which is what upset his fellows. Today, these numbers are known as **irrational numbers.**

92 Sand-sized computers...

can measure the pressure inside an eyeball.

Computer scientists in Michigan, USA, have created a tiny wireless computer, or **mote**, about the size of a grain of sand. It's so small it can fit safely inside a human eye.

The mote was designed to be implanted inside the eyeballs of people suffering from an eye condition called glaucoma.

Layer with pressure and temperature sensors

0.7mm (0.03")

2mm (0.08")

Light-powered battery

The mote measures pressure and temperature in the eye, then communicates that data via radio waves to a computer outside the body.

This helps doctors decide a course of treatment.

Motes that communicate with *each other* form what are known as **smart dust networks**. Computer scientists believe that adding different sensors to motes will soon give these networks hundreds of new uses, such as...

Detecting chemicals in the bloodstream

Measuring air pollution

Measuring salt levels in bridges

(Salty concrete makes bridges unsafe)

93 The brighter the object...

the more negative it becomes.

Negative numbers often describe 'opposite' values on scales. For example, they are used to represent distances below sea level, compared with positive values above sea level. But the brightness of stars uses a topsy-turvy **magnitude** scale in which smaller or more negative numbers represent the brightest objects.

Magnitude is a measure of how brightly an object shines in the sky. In this system, objects with magnitude 1 are 100 times brighter than objects of magnitude 6.

Stars create their own light, but the Moon, planets and man-made objects shine by reflecting light from the Sun.

The Sun: **-27**

Full Moon: **-13**

Sirius: **-1**
Brightest star in night sky

International Space Station: **-3**

Venus: **-4**

Jupiter: **-2**

The Pole Star: **2**

Faintest stars visible to human eye: **6**

Faintest stars visible with binoculars: **10**

This system was developed from a scale invented by Ancient Greek astronomer **Hipparchus** over 2,000 years ago.

Faintest stars visible with powerful telescopes: **25**

Magnitude

-30
-20
-10
0
10
20
30

94 The 7 most wanted problems...

have a price on their heads.

In the year 2000, an international mathematics organization set out the seven biggest mysteries in the math world. They're known as the **Millennium Prize Problems**. Solving any of them would net any mathematical bounty hunter **one million dollars**.

★ WANTED ★

P VS NP PROBLEM

NP-hard

NP complete

NP

P

Wanted since: 1971

Area: Computing

☆★☆ WANTED ☆★☆

Navier–Stokes Equations

$$\frac{\partial u}{\partial t} + \left(u \cdot \nabla \right) u - \nu \nabla^2 u = -\nabla w + g$$

Wanted since: 1800s

Area: Fluid dynamics

REWARD: $1,000,000

WANTED

Hodge Conjecture

Wanted since: 1950

Area: Algebraic geometry

WANTED

Riemann Hypothesis

Wanted since: 1859

Area: Prime numbers

★★ WANTED ★★

POINCARÉ CONJECTURE

PROVED

Wanted since: 1904

Area: 4-D shapes

Claimed in 2003

WANTED

Birch and Swinnerton-Dyer Conjecture

$y^2 = x - x^3$ $y^2 = x^3 - x + 1$

Wanted since: 1965

Area: Number theory

★ WANTED ★

Yang–Mills Existence and Mass Gap

Wanted since: 1970s

Area: Particle physics

REWARD: $1,000,000

Just understanding the problems, let alone finding the solutions, takes mathematicians whole lifetimes.

could lead to a crime spree.

Every time someone buys something online using a credit card, the number on the card is scrambled up so no one can copy and use it. It's safe – but might not be if the **P vs NP Millennium Prize Problem** is ever solved.

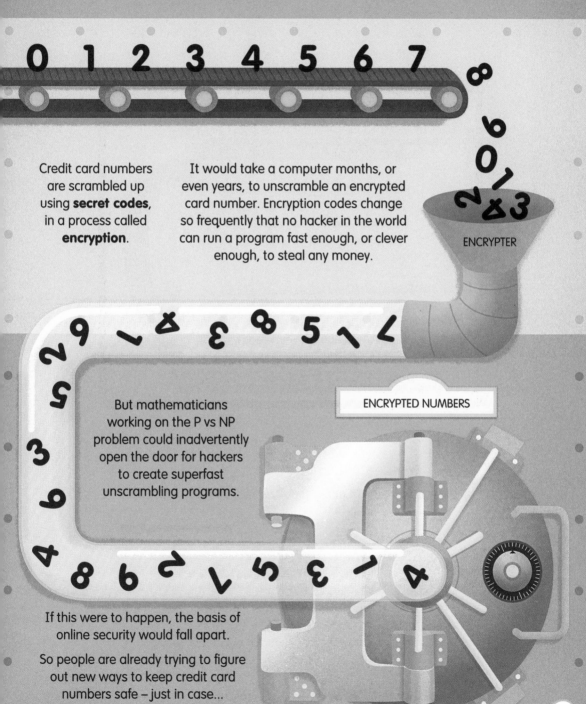

Credit card numbers are scrambled up using **secret codes**, in a process called **encryption**.

It would take a computer months, or even years, to unscramble an encrypted card number. Encryption codes change so frequently that no hacker in the world can run a program fast enough, or clever enough, to steal any money.

ENCRYPTER

ENCRYPTED NUMBERS

But mathematicians working on the P vs NP problem could inadvertently open the door for hackers to create superfast unscrambling programs.

If this were to happen, the basis of online security would fall apart.

So people are already trying to figure out new ways to keep credit card numbers safe – just in case...

96 The webcam was invented...

to watch a pot of coffee.

In 1991, computer scientists at the University of Cambridge had a problem – walking all the way to the kitchen for a coffee, only to find the pot was empty. The solution they came up with led to the development of the first ever **webcam**.

xcoffee

At the time, there was no World Wide Web. Instead, computer scientists **Quentin Stafford-Fraser** and **Paul Jardetzky** wired up a camera from their computers to the office kitchen.

The camera took a picture every two seconds. Using a program called *XCoffee*, everyone in the department could access the pictures through an internal network.

In 1993, a video camera was installed to broadcast the coffee pot live on the web. Anyone could watch it through this first true webcam. Thousands of people around the world tuned in, before it was switched off in 2001.

97 Some numbers are imaginary...

but essential in the real world.

By the 16th century, mathematicians were able to solve equations such as: **if $X^2 = 9$** (X squared, or multiplied by itself, is 9), **then $X = \sqrt{9}$** (X is the square root of 9) **so $X = 3$ or $X = -3$**. But they couldn't find a solution to $X^2 = -9$. How could a number multiplied by itself make a negative number? It didn't make sense – not without a new kind of number.

In 1572, Italian engineer **Rafael Bombelli** described a set of rules for a new system of numbers, which was against all the existing rules of mathematics.

If $X^2 = -1$
then $X = \sqrt{-1}$

This number when multiplied by itself creates a negative number!

But for decades, mathematicians were reluctant to accept these new numbers.

Pah! These numbers are just imaginary!

In 1637, French mathematician **René Descartes** called them **'imaginary'** as an insult.

The term stuck.

Then, in 1777, **Leonard Euler** introduced the symbol **i** to represent imaginary numbers.

If you just start using i, you'll see how useful it is!

$i \times i = -1$
$3i \times 2i = -6$

Fiddlesticks! It's just gobbledygook.

In time, mathematicians realized that imaginary numbers allowed them to find a complete set of solutions to complicated equations. This had many practical uses, such as designing bridges and electric circuits.

ran entirely on water.

In 1936, an engineer named Vladimir Lukyanov built a computer that could solve complicated equations. Where digital computers today use electronics, this one used water flowing through hundreds of glass tubes.

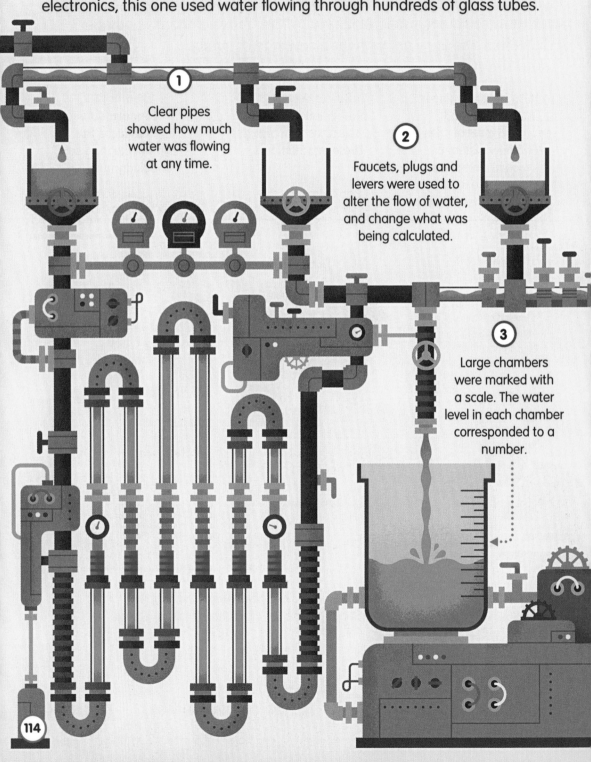

1 Clear pipes showed how much water was flowing at any time.

2 Faucets, plugs and levers were used to alter the flow of water, and change what was being calculated.

3 Large chambers were marked with a scale. The water level in each chamber corresponded to a number.

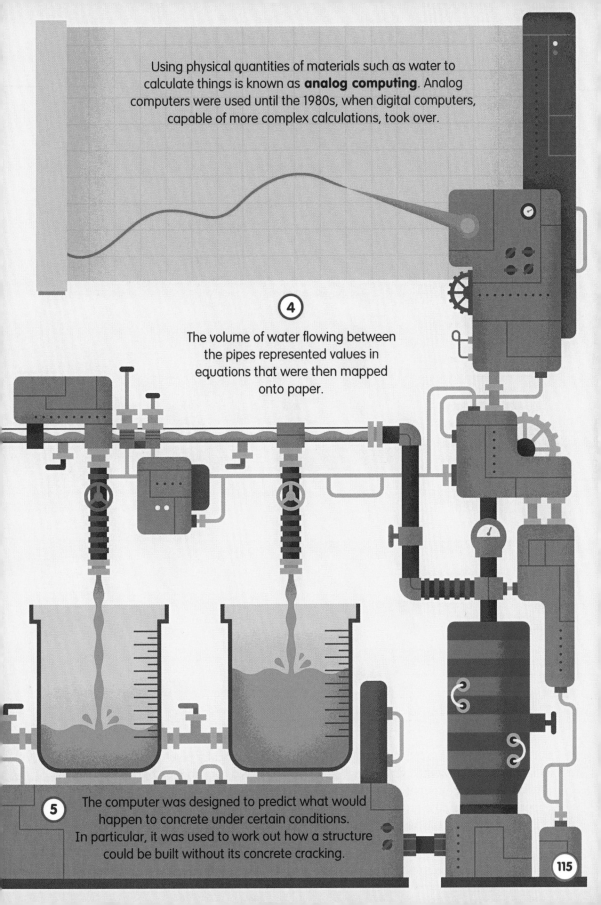

Using physical quantities of materials such as water to calculate things is known as **analog computing**. Analog computers were used until the 1980s, when digital computers, capable of more complex calculations, took over.

4

The volume of water flowing between the pipes represented values in equations that were then mapped onto paper.

5

The computer was designed to predict what would happen to concrete under certain conditions. In particular, it was used to work out how a structure could be built without its concrete cracking.

99 A Danish king's legacy...
lives on in wireless communication.

Bluetooth® wireless technology allows computers and electronic devices to exchange data, such as photos, music and videos, using radio waves. It got its name from the 10th-century Danish king, **Harald 'Bluetooth' Gormsson**.

King Harald is famous for uniting tribes from separate regions into one nation, now known as Denmark.

Nobody knows for sure how he got his nickname. One legend has it, he ate so many blueberries, one of his teeth turned blue.

Harald's initials, written in old Danish letters, or **runes**

Bluetooth wireless technology connects different devices to one another. Harald brought groups of people together. The technology's inventors noticed this similarity, so named it after him.

The symbol for Bluetooth wireless technology is a combination of Harald's initials:

$$\text{ᚼ} + \text{ᛒ} = \text{❈}®$$

100 Being forgotten online...

is a human right. Or is it?

The internet is used by billions of people every day, but no one owns it and no one controls it. That means it's up to everyone to decide on the rules of the internet, and to ask important questions about what you should and shouldn't do online.

Whose responsibility is it to keep people safe from dangerous or offensive things online?

Search engines? Individual websites? Parents, caregivers and teachers? Governments?

Is access to the internet a universal human right?

This is known as digital rights. In some countries it's already law that everyone should have access to the internet.

Can I post whatever I like online?

Some people argue everyone has freedom of speech and should be able to say what they like, but others think offensive views shouldn't be shared.

Is the internet policed?

Not really, but a lot of websites are monitored regularly, and offensive or criminal content is removed.

Should I be allowed to have mentions of me on the internet permanently deleted, so they don't unfairly affect my life?

This is known as the 'right to be forgotten', and was made a legal right in the European Union in 2006. But it's not a legal right everywhere, and it's still controversial.

Should governments be allowed to control what I see on the internet?

Limiting what citizens of a country can see online is called 'censorship'.

Timeline

2,500 years ago
Ancient Greek scholar Pythagoras set up a school of numbers.

2,300 years ago
Ancient Babylonians used zero to help describe large numbers.

2,200 years ago
Ancient Greek warriors used **scytales** to send coded military messages.

1,400 years ago
Indian mathematician Brahmagupta was the first to define **zero** as a number.

1670s
Calculus was invented by scientist Isaac Newton... ...and mathematician Gottfried Leibniz.

1792
French surveyors measured part of the Earth's circumference to help define a new measurement: the meter.

1843
English countess Ada Lovelace wrote out the oldest known computer program, using holes punched into a card.

1873
Typewriter manufacturers created a new order for English letters: **QWERTY**.

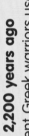
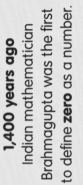
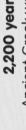

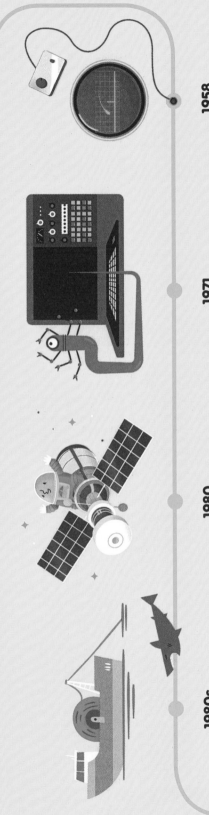

1958
Players enjoyed the first two-player electronic computer game.

1971
The world's first computer virus was released on the ARPANET – and fixed.

1980
Satellites in orbit helped set up GPS – Global Positioning System.

1980s
The first undersea fiber-optic internet cables were laid.

2008
300,000 couples married on 08/08/08, the luckiest date in China's history.

2000
$1,000,000 was promised to whoever solves any of seven 'Millennium Prize' math problems.

1991
British computer scientist Tim Berners-Lee made the World Wide Web publicly available.

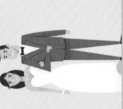

2009
The first cryptocurrencies were created.

Glossary

This glossary explains some of the words used in this book. Words written in *italic* type have their own entries.

analog computer A computer that uses quantities of physical materials, such as water or stone counters, to make calculations.

ARPANET A network of 28 computers created by the US Defense Department in the late 1960s. It's considered to be a forerunner of the *internet*.

artificial intelligence The ability of a computer to perform tasks that usually require human intelligence.

binary code A *code* that uses two symbols, 0 and 1, to communicate information.

bit A single unit of *data* stored in a computer, represented as a 0 or 1 in a piece of *binary code*.

bitcoin A *digital* currency, or *cryptocurrency*, that was invented in 1997.

bot A piece of *software* that can run on its own.

bot herder A *hacker* that illegally installs *software* on other computers to gain control over them.

bug An error in a piece of computer *software* or *hardware*.

byte A unit for measuring the amount of *data* in a computer *file* or *program*. One byte is a set of eight *bits* in a string of *binary code*. A million bytes is a megabyte.

calculus The branch of mathematics used to describe how things change over time.

cartesian coordinates Numbers used to show the location of a point relative to fixed lines, or axes.

cipher A secret message written in an *encoded* language.

code
(noun) Any system of signs or symbols, such as letters and numbers, that communicates a message. Secret codes are often created to communicate secret information. 'Computer code' is the general term for the *programming languages* used to write a *program*.
(verb) The act of writing a computer *program*.

compiler A *program* that converts computer *code* into a language known as *machine code*, so that a computer can understand it.

computer A device that can store, retrieve, and process *data* by following a *program*.

computer vision The science that aims to give computers the ability to interpret images and videos like humans.

constant A number or letter in an *equation* with a value that doesn't change.

control flow The order in which instructions in a *program* are carried out.

cryptocurrency A purely *digital* currency that uses *encryption* techniques to create more of it, and to transfer it securely.

cryptography The study of *codes* and how to decipher them.

data In a computer, all of the information needed for a *program* to run. It's most often stored as *electrons* inside the computer's *hardware*.

database A collection of *data* stored in a computer.

digital Involving or related to the use of computer technology. It also describes anything that is stored or communicated as *bits*, or a machine that stores information as bits.

dimension A measurement used to describe the amount of space an object takes up. For example, length, width and depth.

document A piece of text or graphics, often stored as a *file* on a computer.

electron One of the types of tiny particle that make up atoms, the building blocks of all solids, liquids and gases. *Data* in most computers is stored as electrons.

email A message sent electronically from one computer to another, short for 'electronic mail'.

encode To translate information into a coded language, or express it in a different form.

encryption A security measure that reorders information to prevent unauthorized access.

equation A mathematical statement that says that two amounts or values are the same. For example, $x + 3y = 12$.

file A set of *data* that has been saved on a computer and given its own name.

formula A type of *equation* that shows the relationship between two or more *variables*.

fraction A number that can be written as a proportion of two *integers*, such as ½ or ¾. They fall between integers on a number line.

geometry The branch of mathematics that describes shapes, points, lines, angles and *dimensions*.

glitch A sudden problem, for example in a machine or piece of *software*, that stops something from working properly.

hacker A person who tries to break into a computer system without permission, often in order to gather confidential information.

hardware The physical parts of a computer that carry out the instructions given by the *software*.

hertz The unit for measuring the speed at which a computer carries out operations.

imaginary number A number that gives a *negative number* when *squared*.

infinity The state of being infinite, or immeasurable. A number that is infinite goes on forever, and can never be given a specific value.

integer A number not followed by *fractions* or decimals, also known as a 'whole number'.

internet A vast network of computer networks that allows computer users to connect to other computer users.

irrational number Any number that cannot be reached by dividing an *integer* by another *integer*, meaning that it cannot be written as an *integer* or *fraction*.

machine code The language all *programs* are translated into before a computer can carry out the instructions.

magnitude The size or extent of something, such as the brightness of a star or the strength of an earthquake, relative to a fixed value.

mathematical proof A statement that shows that a mathematical rule or *theorem* is definitely true.

microchip A small piece of metal inside a computer that holds large amounts of *data* and performs specified tasks.

negative number A number that is less than zero.

online Connected to, or accessible through, the *internet*.

packet A block of *data* sent across the *internet*.

paradox A statement or idea that contradicts itself, such as "this sentence is a lie."

pixel A small square on a computer screen that is filled with color and combined with other pixels to form images on a screen.

power The raised number in a calculation such as 10^3 that tells you the number of times to multiply the other number by itself.

prime number A number that can only be divided by itself and 1 to give an *integer*.

probability The branch of mathematics that calculates the likelihood that something will happen, or happened in the past.

program A set of step-by-step instructions, written in computer *code*, that tells a computer what to do.

programmer A person who writes computer *programs* for a living.

programming language A language *programmers* use to write *programs*. There are thousands of them.

quantum computer A type of computer that relies on the motion and properties of the particles that make up atoms to store and process *data*.

qubit The basic unit of information in a *quantum computer*, short for 'quantum *bit*'.

Random Access Memory (RAM) The part of a computer that stores the *data* being used by the computer at that moment.

rational number Any number that can be expressed as a *fraction* or an *integer*.

scale A range of values used as a system for measuring or grading something.

search engine A *program* that searches the *internet* for *web pages* containing a particular word searched for by a user.

sequence An ordered series of numbers that follows set rules.

software A set of programs that allow computer users to perform specific tasks or activities, such as playing a game or writing a document.

spam irrelevant or unwanted messages sent over the *internet*, often for the purposes of advertizing or spreading *viruses*.

square (verb) To multiply a number by itself.

square root A number that is squared is known as the 'square root' of the product. For example, the square root of 4 is 2, because 2 squared equals 4.

super-computer A particularly powerful computer that can process large amounts of *data* very quickly.

technological singularity A hypothetical moment in the future, when *artificial intelligence* irreversibly surpasses that of humans.

theorem A rule that can be proved true through step-by-step logical reasoning.

transistor A small component in an electronic device that controls the flow of electricity. Transistors in a computer store *data*.

variable An element in an *equation* that can change in value.

viral When a video, image, article or post spreads quickly and widely to hundreds of thousands of people via the *internet*, it is described as going 'viral'.

virtual Created by a computer to appear to exist.

virus A type of germ that can cause disease. A computer virus is a harmful *program* that enters a computer system and changes or destroys the *data* stored there.

wearable An item of clothing with built-in computer technology.

webcam A camera that transmits still or moving images over the *internet*, often in real time.

web page An *online document* designed to be viewed as part of a *website*.

website A set of *web pages* that share the same name.

World Wide Web A vast network of *websites* that can be accessed over the *internet*.

zombie A computer taken over by a *bot herder*.

Index

Internet links

For links to websites where you can discover more surprising facts about numbers, computers and coding, with video clips, quizzes and activities, go to the Usborne Quicklinks website at **www.usborne.com/quicklinks** and enter the keywords: **things to know about numbers**.

Here are some of the things you can do at the websites we recommend:

- discover how to count to over 1,000 on your fingers
- play chess against a computer
- meet an artist who uses code to make art
- see ways the Fibonacci sequence appears in nature
- try some simple coding projects of your own

Please follow the online safety guidelines at the Usborne Quicklinks website. We recommend that children are supervised while using the internet.

Usborne Publishing is not responsible and does not accept liability for the availability or content of any website other than its own, or for any exposure to harmful, offensive or inaccurate material which may appear on the Web. Usborne Publishing will have no liability for any damage or loss caused by viruses that may be downloaded as a result of browsing the sites it recommends.

Acknowledgements

With thanks to MolecularExpressions at Florida State University (p. 36), D-Wave Systems Inc. (p. 95), Thalmic Labs Inc., Erik De Nijs of Nieuwe Heren, and CUTECIRCUIT (p. 104-105) for permission to include their products in this book. The Bluetooth word mark and logos (p. 116) are registered trademarks and are owned by Bluetooth SIG, Inc.

To dig up 100 incredible facts...

takes a team of intrepid miners.

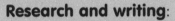

Research and writing:
Alice James, Eddie Reynolds, Minna Lacey,
Rose Hall and Alex Frith

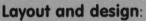

Layout and design:
Lenka Hrehova, Freya Harrison,
Tilly Kitching and Jenny Offley

Series editor:
Ruth Brocklehurst

US editor:
Carrie Armstrong

Series designer:
Stephen Moncrieff

Illustration:
Federico Mariani and Parko Polo
Additional illustration by Shaw Nielsen

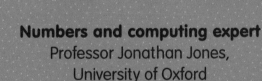

Numbers and computing expert
Professor Jonathan Jones,
University of Oxford